THE
BATTLE
OF RESACA

THE BATTLE OF RESACA

Atlanta Campaign
1864

by

Philip L. Secrist

Mercer University Press
Macon, Georgia
1998

The paper used in this publication meets the minimum require-
ments of American National Standard for Permanence of Paper for
Printed Library Materials ANSI Z39.48–1984.

Library of Congress Cataloging-in-Publication Data

Secrist, Philip L.
Battle of Resaca : Atlanta Campaign, 1864 / Philip L. Secrist.
p. cm.
Includes bibliographical references (p.) and index.
ISBN 0-86554-601-0 (alk. paper)
1. Resaca, Battle of, 1864. I. Title.
E476.7.S33   1998
973.7'36—dc21

TABLE OF CONTENTS

LIST OF MAPS AND ILLUSTRATIONS

A SPECIAL DEDICATION

To my beloved companion in life, Kay Kimsey Secrist, who read this manuscript and suggested valuable improvements in the text, and to sons Jim and Scott, and long-time friends Robert Crowe and Henry Higgins, who have shared with me the many years of battlefield "digs" and the good times that go with them—THANKS FOR THE HELP AND THE MEMORIES!!

The Battle of Resaca in May 1864 marked the first heavy engagement of the Atlanta Campaign; forced the Confederate Army of Tennessee from its formidable positions outside Dalton, Georgia; and served as a precursor in tactics and results of most of the succeeding battles through that fateful summer, culminating in the encirclement of Atlanta by Sherman's Union forces, the bloody Confederate attempts to break the siege, and the ultimate surrender of Atlanta on September 2, 1864. While noted and discussed in many volumes on the Atlanta campaign, both by participants and historians, Resaca has not received the concentrated treatment which is its due. Dr. Philip Secrist's book on the battle accordingly constitutes a welcome addition to the historiography of the Atlanta Campaign. Dr. Secrist first published his account of the battle in his article for the Spring 1978 *Atlanta Historical Society Journal.* The present volume has been enhanced by four color maps and additional materials contributed by Dr. Secrist, including significant discoveries on the battlefield.

The effective surprise of the Confederate forces by the appearance of McPherson's Army of the Tennessee through Snake Creek Gap in the rear of the Confederate fortifications around Dalton, the Union troops failure to exploit their advantage, the uncoordinated attacks and counterattacks by units of both commands, the battle over the guns on Simonson's Battery, so typical of that era, are all covered astutely by Dr. Secrist, as are Sherman's deficiencies as a commander of troops in battle which were again displayed at Resaca. The southward retreat from Resaca along the Western and Atlantic Railroad by Johnston's Army of Tennessee as a result of the Union flanking maneuvers was to be repeated during the rest of the summer until the fortifications of Atlanta were reached.

A man of many talents, Dr. Secrist is a noted Civil War artifact and relic hunter and collector. A past president of the Atlanta Civil War Roundtable, he currently serves as chairman of the Georgia Civil War Commission, dedicated to the preservation of Civil War battle sites in the state, and the Resaca Battlefield is high on the list of its priorities. In addition, Dr. Secrist, an associate professor of history at Kennesaw State University served as the duly elected chairman of the Cobb County Commission, ably presiding over its growth from 1988 to 1992.

Mercer University Press is pleased to publish *Resaca*.

Tom Watson Brown
Chairman, Mercer University Press

FOREWORD

I was a high school history teacher in the Atlanta Public Schools when I made my first trip to the Resaca battlefield in the spring of 1958. My interest in the battlefields of the Civil War had begun two years earlier with a visit to Leggetts Hill in Atlanta, the site of the Battle of Atlanta, July 22, 1864. Here in a weed-filled vacant lot on the slope of an unmarked historic hillside, I picked up my first handful of battlefield relics. For me, the thrill of this experience led directly to a lifetime quest for military information about the American Civil War. Two years later, with my personal copy of the *Official Records* (Atlanta Campaign, Volume 38), and a collection of maps of the Resaca battle site "tucked under my arm," I arrived at the Resaca battlefield. On that day my metal detecting equipment (a World War II mine detector) was really not needed—in Resaca in 1958 artillery shell fragments littered the ground.

From that day forward for thirty years I was a frequent visitor to the Resaca battlefield. During the construction of Interstate 75 in 1960 I was present almost every sunny weekend witnessing a rather substantial destruction of portions of the battlefield at the south end of the battle site in "Bishop-General" Leonidas Polk's front. The construction of the interchange here at I-75 and SR 136 required the removal of several small battlefield hills; the loss of which has been compounded by the absence of any significant archeological record at this point on the field. By 1978, my interest in Resaca prompted me to share with others these years of field and archival study. My work at Western Reserve Historical Library, and in the Jacob D. Cox collection in the manuscript division of the Ohio State Archives in Columbus, Ohio was useful. And my study in the Wilbur Kurtz collection at the Atlanta Historical Society, with some research at the University of Georgia, led me to a number of special collections of diaries and papers associated with the Resaca battle site. Kennesaw Mountain National Battlefield Park's small but valuable collection also proved quite useful. The article which resulted from these efforts is entitled, "Resaca: For Sherman a Moment of Truth." It was published in the Spring 1978 issue of *The Atlanta Historical Journal* (Vol. XXII, Number 1). *Part I* of this book is substantially a reprinting of the 1978 article with improved mapping and illustrations. There are also certain clarifications and additions that have been made to the original text.

Part II of this book explores some of the postwar events concerning the field of battle at Resaca. Abandoned by the armies in 1864, subsequently returning to its previous agricultural and pastoral uses, there would be many scars on countryside and human spirit to heal. The Resaca community could never entirely forget its brush with history. Military entrenchments were everywhere extending through forest and field, rusting iron and tin from battle and camp littered the landscape, and the ever-present oxidizing lead "minie" ball covered the recently plowed cornfields like hail from a storm. The occasional discovery of human remains was a macabre reminder of the personal tragedy concealed in some forgotten battlefield grave. All these experiences make for a keen community awareness regarding its past—the sense of a common historical bond passed down from generation to generation. The village of Resaca in Gordon County, Georgia, is one such place.

Resaca's rich heritage, and the preservation of its past, began to converge with the introduction of legislation in 1993 to create a state historical commission dedicated to the preservation of Civil War sites along the hundred-mile corridor of the Atlanta Campaign of 1864. This bill entitled "Atlanta Campaign Commission" was passed by the Georgia Senate. Forwarded to the House, it was sent through the Rules Committee to the House floor for the vote. At this point Representative John Carlisle of Griffin, Georgia persuaded the House Rules Committee to allow him to substitute a broader bill so as to create a Georgia Civil War Commission. Senator Johnny Issackson, sponsor of the Senate version of the bill (accompanied by Phil Secrist, originator of the idea for an Atlanta Campaign Commission in Georgia) met in conference with Representative Carlisle and agreed, with some minor changes, to support the Carlisle bill. In this manner the Georgia Civil War Commission was created. For the historic field of battle at Resaca and the scores of other deserving wartime sites around the state, and for thousands of heritage-minded people in Georgia, the creation of this Civil War Commission was a major step toward the practical realization of many deserving Civil War historic preservation activities.

Resaca was to be among the first beneficiaries of the preservation energies of the Georgia Civil War Commission. In 1994, led by John Carlisle, the Commission made contact with representatives of an estate willing to sell a 1200-acre tract of historic property in the heart of the battlefield. In the more than two years since negotiations began, with frustrations in the matter ebbing and flowing, Commission members Dr. Eugene Hatfield, John Carlisle, Dr. Phil Secrist, Oliver Keller, Dr. Elizabeth Lyon, and Louise Smith became especially involved in promoting support for the Resaca acquisition. These individuals took leadership roles in soliciting land acquisition funding from public and private sources. During this time research and preservation planning work was conducted at the Resaca battle site with the aid of several generous study grants. Governor Zell Miller and the Georgia State Legislature included $500,000 seed money in the 1994 state budget for the purpose of Civil War battle site acquisition. Commissioner Lonice Barrett, director of the Georgia Department of Natural Resources, along with Mark Edwards, Director of the Historic Preservation Divisions (who also serves as State Historic Preservation Officer) have declared the Resaca site their "number one priority." Today, June 1997, with this consensus by state officials, and with the generous outpouring of acquisition funding from several major private foundations, the people of Georgia are nearing the moment of a very major triumph in the preservation of America's Civil War heritage. The following publication is dedicated to the prospect of this preservation achievement.

Philip L. Secrist, Member
Georgia Civil War Commission

SPECIAL ACKNOWLEDGMENT

In 1995 steps were taken by several individuals in the Resaca community to organize a local support group to work with the Georgia Civil War Commission in setting aside a portion of the Resaca battlefield dedicated to the memory of those soldiers, Yank and Reb, who had fought on these fields in 1864. Among those leading the way in creating "Friends of the Resaca Battlefield" was Resaca Mayor Joe Don Griffith, and locals Kenneth Padgett, and Jule Medders. Padgett is a former policeman who is an officer in the local chapter of the Sons of Confederate Veterans. Medders is a musician and former school teacher whose family owns significant portions of the Resaca battlefield including the site of the famed Four Gun Battery. Mayor Griffith's family has been in the community for several generations. In addition to his many official duties, Griffith's interests include the organizing and promoting of the annual reenactment of the Battle of Resaca now in its fourteenth year. The Resaca reenactment attracts many participants and large numbers of visitors.

The "Friends of the Resaca Battlefield" is officially organized with by-laws and charter. Meetings are held regularly, a monthly newsletter is published, new memberships are actively solicited, and annual membership fees required. A typical meeting agenda includes a program focused on area Civil War history, preservation goals, or historical conservation strategies. Attendance at these meetings varies between twenty and fifty, and fund raising is conducted from time to time in the community. On a recent occasion the "Friends" organization contributed $1000 to the Resaca battlefield acquisition fund. Indicative of the general interest in the community in the Resaca battlefield preservation effort, the Resaca city council recently approved a $2000 contribution to the same fund. Thus today, through its energies and its pocketbook the community of Resaca continues to demonstrate its commitment to a sense of heritage—a contemporary bonding with a rich historical past!

PART I

Conduct of Battle

General William T. Sherman, West Point graduate, personal friend of Ulysses S. Grant, commanded the Federal forces in the Atlanta Campaign in 1864. After the Resaca battle, Sherman's 100,000-man army became a hard marching force of foot soldiers who delivered in a politically timely fashion the capture of Atlanta on September 2 to a grateful President.

Gen. Joseph E. Johnston commanded the Confederate Army of Tennessee in the Atlanta Campaign until relieved from command in mid-July by Jefferson Davis, Confederate president. Loved by the soldiers he commanded, Johnston's removal from command resulted in widespread shock and disappointment among the rank and file in the army.

Johnston's skillful defense against a foe that outnumbered the Confederates almost two-to-one earned the respect of Sherman. The two became good friends after the war. Johnston served as an honorary pallbearer at Sherman's funeral in 1891; standing hatless in a freezing rain, he contracted pneumonia and died a month later.

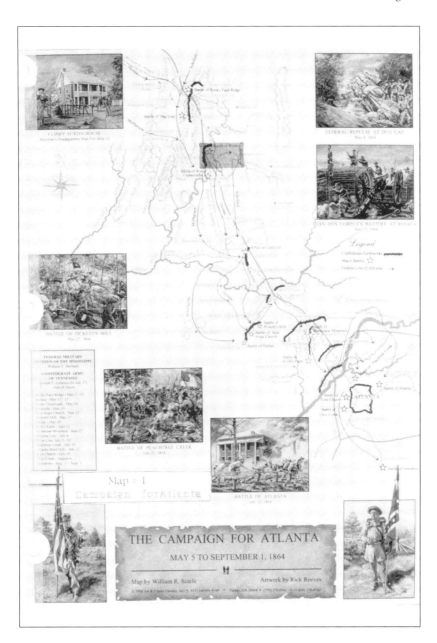

Map #1
Campaign for Atlanta

CHAPTER 1

The Plan of Battle

As William T. Sherman's armies broke camp and swung down the roads past Tunnel Hill and Villanow toward Dalton and Resaca, the woods and fields provided a pleasant setting for the military pageant streaming south. It was Spring, 1864, as the two northern armies, one in Georgia, the other in Virginia, embarked on what would be the final act in the mighty struggle to preserve the Union.

In its basic scheme, Sherman's plan in Georgia was quite simple. With his much larger Federal army, he would crush Joseph E. Johnston's Confederates near Chattanooga. Without a defending army, the occupation of Atlanta would quickly follow, and with its capture, the will to continue the struggle to destroy the Union would cease in the deep South. Tactically, the plan was to force the Confederate Army of Tennessee to give battle near Chattanooga by confronting it with the Army of the Cumberland, the largest of Sherman's three grand armies, while the Army of the Ohio and the Army of the Tennessee, smaller Union armies under Sherman's general command, would function as a pair of highly mobile forces slashing at the flanks and rear of the opponent, pinning the Confederates in a crushing embrace.[1]

The key to the campaign to capture Atlanta was transportation. Without the railroad connecting Chattanooga with Atlanta, Sherman's army could not have been adequately supplied. The Atlanta Campaign in a daily practical sense became a contest for control of the Western and Atlantic Railroad. In Sherman's words:

> The Atlanta Campaign of 1864 would have been impossible without this road, that all our battles were fought for its possession, and that the Western and Atlantic Railroad of Georgia should be the pride of every true American because by reason of its existence the Union was saved. Every foot of it should be sacred ground,

because it was moistened by patriotic blood, and that over a hundred miles of it was fought a continuous battle of 120 days, during which, day and night, were heard the continuous boom of cannon and the sharp crack of the rifle.[2]

Resaca was to be the first important contest for that railroad.

The key to the plan, of course, was to force the battle near Chattanooga, where great stockpiles of Federal supplies lay immediately available and secure behind Lookout Mountain and Missionary Ridge. Sherman knew that Johnston would seek to weaken his Federal foe by drawing the Union armies deep into the interior where a crippling blow might be struck—every mile nearer Atlanta would increase Sherman's vulnerability. (See Map#1, "Campaign for Atlanta.")

A study of his maps convinced Sherman that the great battle for Atlanta should take place somewhere north of Rome, Georgia. While the two armies would probably make first contact near Johnston's winter camp at Dalton, Sherman knew that the high ridge called Rocky Face and the deep gorge through it known as Mill Creek Gap (the only approach to Johnston's position that would not expose Sherman's supply center at Chattanooga) ruled out Dalton as the place for the great contest. Some weeks before, General George H. Thomas, who commanded the Army of the Cumberland, alerted Sherman to the opportunities offered by Snake Creek Gap as a route by which the railroad could be reached at Resaca and Johnston's position turned.[3] Thomas had offered to lead his Cumberland soldiers through this defile while the armies of the Ohio and the Tennessee occupied Johnston's attention at Dalton. Sherman saw the merit in the plan, but because he distrusted Thomas' ability to move his large army rapidly through the gorge, and because of unexpected transportation delays to the Army of the Tennessee units of which were en route from Mississippi, he decided to modify the plan to reverse the roles of the Cumberland and Tennessee armies. James B. McPherson's Army of the Tennessee was to strike quickly near Resaca—his movements screened by the high ridges west of Dalton, while the Army of the Cumberland was to remain near Dalton and engage in diversionary tactics.[4]

If the plan was to succeed in bringing the Confederates to bay on favorable terrain, McPherson must entrench across the railroad somewhere north of Calhoun. Johnston's communications would thus be cut, and the Confederate commander must then either attack or seek retreat to Atlanta far to the east in rugged hills. "I will secure the Tunnel Hill," Sherman wired General-in-Chief Ulysses S. Grant on May 4, "then throw McPherson rapidly on his (Johnston's) communications, attacking at the same time in front cautiously and in force."[5] (See Map #2) McPherson with 20,000 infantry was to leave his camps near Rossville, Georgia, on May 5 and in a rapid march sweep around the enemy's left via Villanow and Ship's Gap, and secure the pass at Snake Creek near Resaca by May 7. From this position at Snake Creek Gap, a bold attack could easily be made at any point on the rail line in the vicinity of Resaca. All that was needed was speed and some audacity. Should Johnston fall back along the railroad, "make the most of the opportunity by the most vigorous attack possible," Sherman wrote McPherson on May 5, "as it may save us what we have most reason to apprehend—a slow pursuit, in which he gains strength as we lose it."[6] The events of the next few days would serve to remind the northern commander of his own deficiencies, and of the limitations of key subordinates. Cumulatively, their mistakes would produce a parade of missed opportunities that would force William Tecumseh Sherman to revise his plan for the months ahead. It would be a long road to Atlanta.

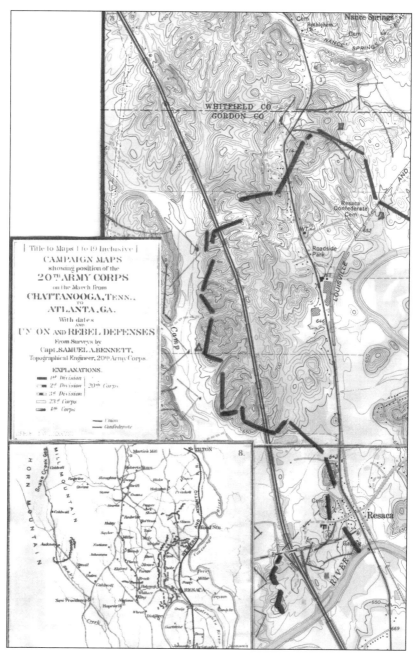

Map #2
Resaca Field of Battle.

CHAPTER 2

First Try for Resaca

The rough and hilly farmland around Resaca was interspersed in 1864 with thick underbrush.[7] Slicing through this landscape, the Western and Atlantic Railroad crossed the Oostanaula River at Resaca on its journey north from Atlanta to Chattanooga. The village had been named by the workers who constructed the railroad in the 1850s, some of whom were veterans of the battle of Resaca de la Palma in the Mexican War. By 1864 Resaca had grown to only a few dozen structures clustered about the freight station. Small farms dotted the surrounding countryside (see Map #3), and west of town lay a narrow valley through which flowed Camp Creek and its tributaries. Southwest of the village the creek emptied into the Oostanaula River. Hills and ridges of medium ruggedness formed a border to this valley, following generally a north-south pattern and conforming roughly with the flow of the creek. About a mile north of the village, the railroad swept sharply off to the east where it paralleled for a short distance the southward-flowing Conasauga River—a broad stream that joins the Coosawattee just east of town, the two forming the Oostanaula and flowing as one on their westward journey, skirting the village on the south. Some three miles north of the Resaca depot, the railroad again resumes its northerly route to Tilton, Dalton, and beyond. It was in this rectangle formed by the creek and the rivers, and dissected by the railroad, that the battle of Resaca was fought May 14 and 15, 1864. (See Map #3).

Resaca, the great battle with which Sherman hoped to conclude the campaign, began to develop on the evening of May 7 when Johnston received information from cavalry pickets at Ship's Gap of the presence of at least a division of enemy at LaFayette, a small town just west of the picket post. Fearing that Sherman intended to strike the Confederate rear at Rome, Johnston instructed his cavalry to

Polk's main line of infantry and artillery fortifications was anchored at the river a few hundred yards west of the railroad bridge at the western edge of town. Polk's right flank connected with Hardee's on the hills bordering Camp Creek a short distance north of Resaca near present-day I-75. This primary line of defense was never attacked by federal infantry forces, but did serve as a staging point late in the day on May 14th for several counterattacks by Polk in his unsuccessful effort to recapture the group of small hills bordering the eastern banks of Camp Creek which had been lost to Logan's federal forces a few hours earlier.

The Georgia historical marker on the east bank of Camp Creek near the SR136 overpass at I-75, and the one at the intersection of SR136 and the old Resaca road (west side of Bald Hill) are misleading, suggesting that Polk's main line of defense was at Bald Hill and that it had been captured, forcing Polk to construct principal defenses near town. Actually, we learn from the *Official Records* and from the field maps from the *Official Atlas* (see this page) there was no Confederate battle line on Bald Hill, and the Confederate infantry position on the Camp Creek east hills which was overrun on the 14th was mostly undermanned, disconnected rifle pits. Polk's principal battle line was always near town and had been constructed several days before the battle commenced.

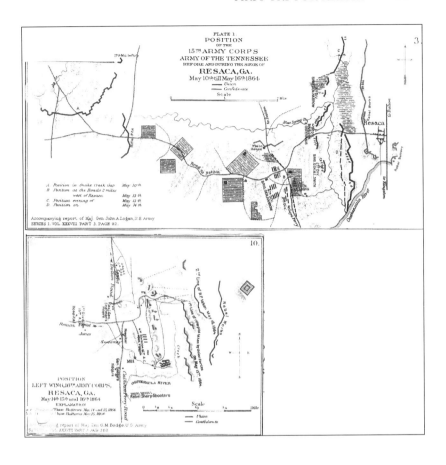

PLATE 1.
POSITION
OF THE
15ᵀᴴ ARMY CORPS
ARMY OF THE TENNESSEE
BEFORE AND DURING THE SIEGE OF
RESACA, GA.
May 10ᵗʰ till May 16ᵗʰ 1864.

A. Position in Snake Creek Gap   May 10ᵗʰ
B. Position at the Roads 2 miles
    west of Resaca   May 13ᵗʰ
C. Position evening of   May 13ᵗʰ
D. Position on   May 14ᵗʰ

Accompanying report of Maj. Gen. John A. Logan, U.S. Army
SERIES 1. VOL. XXXVIII PART 3. PAGE 82.

POSITION
LEFT WING, 16ᵀᴴ ARMY CORPS,
RESACA, GA.
May 14ᵗʰ 15ᵗʰ and 16ᵗʰ 1864
EXPLANATION

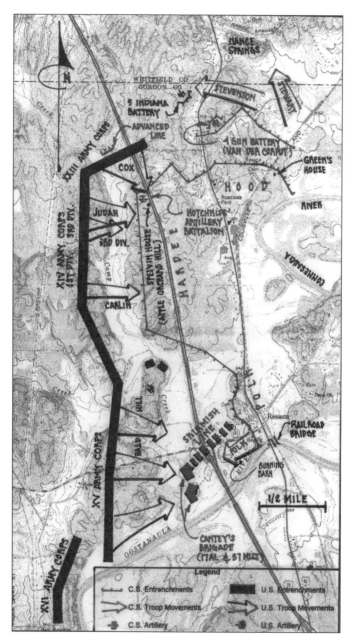

Map #3
Troop Positions, Resaca Battlefield
May 14 & 15, 1864

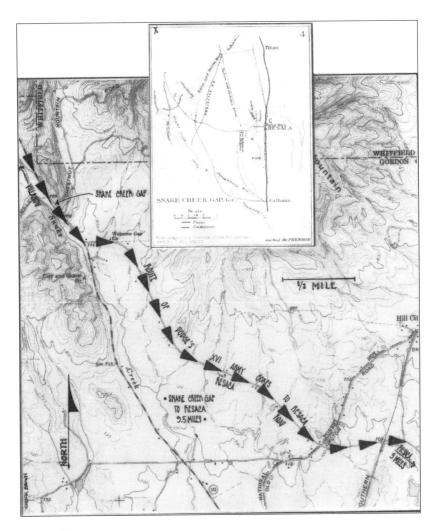

Map #4
Federal Approach to Resaca via Snake Creek Gap
May 9, 1864

guard the railroad from Rome northward to Calhoun. Further to secure the railroad, Johnston ordered Major General William M. Loring's division, vanguard of the approaching Mississippi army under Leonidas Polk to support the two regiments of James Cantey's brigade previously ordered to Resaca on May 5.[8] But by May 9 when Grenville Dodge's 10,000-man 16th Corps of McPherson's Federal infantry appeared at Resaca, only Cantey's two regiments, unseasoned soldiers fresh from garrison duty at Mobile, reinforced by a small brigade of cavalry under Colonel J. Warren Grigsby, stood ready to defend the Confederates' crucial lifeline.[9] (See Map #4, next page)

As the advance of the 16th Corps moved down the Resaca road on May 9, they were attacked by the Confederate cavalry. So vigorous was this attack that the leading units of Union cavalry and its supporting infantry had to be deployed before the advance could resume. The mission of the 16th Corps, as Dodge understood it, was to press up close to Resaca while other troops farther north cut the railroad.[10] Actually, there were no forces in position to strike the railroad between Resaca and Dalton. John Logan's 15th Corps, the nearest unit, was assigned to follow Dodge's corps to Resaca in a support capacity, and the attack made a few miles north at Dug Gap the day before was intended to do nothing more than divert attention from the blow aimed at Resaca.[11] The confusion as to Dodge's purpose on May 9 was partly the result of the misunderstanding between McPherson and Sherman. McPherson understood his instructions from Sherman to mean that the railroad was to be cut if possible, and then fall back and take a strong defensive position in Snake Creek Gap. Sherman, on the other hand, intended that McPherson should make a bold effort to break the railroad and entrench across it, retreating to the safety of the gap only if pressed by overwhelming numbers.[12]

Aside from the stubborn Confederate cavalry, there was little to impede the heavy columns of Dodge's infantry. The countryside through which the Federal soldiers moved was densely wooded. There were few houses along the road to Resaca, and the women and children who remained in these homes could tell Dodge very little about the strength of the Confederate forces in the village ahead. As the advance neared Resaca, the opposition stiffened. Atop a bald hill just west of Camp Creek, Cantey's 37th Mississippi regiment prepared to receive the rapidly advancing host. It was a futile hope, of course, for when Dodge reinforced his skirmish line with four regiments, supported by artillery and three additional brigades of infantry and charged the Mississippians, the southern lines were quickly overwhelmed and driven, routed and confused, across the creek and into the fortifications at Resaca. Nineteen prisoners from the 37th Mississippi were captured, and a commanding position on the west side of Camp Creek within musket range of the village was achieved. All seemed ready for the final assault on a demoralized and greatly outnumbered foe near the railroad scarcely half a mile away.[13]

With Bald Hill occupied and McPherson personally present, Dodge ordered a group of mounted men (all the available cavalry) to reconnoiter the country north and east to determine the most feasible approach to the railroad. Striking the main wagon road north of Resaca, this small band proceeded up the road toward Dalton and managed to reach the railroad just north of Resaca about two miles south of Tilton. Here they succeeded in burning a wood station, cutting the telegraph wire, and destroying a short section of the track. Since the railroad was heavily patrolled by Confederate cavalry, however, little else was accomplished, and the mounted troops returned to Dodge shortly after dark.[14]

Meanwhile, McPherson ordered Dodge to defend Bald Hill at the creek with one division, while a second division probed eastward for the railroad. Pivoting on the left flank of the force at the hill, James C. Veatch, leading this second division north and east across the nearest forks of Camp Creek, reached the open fields east of the stream.[15] Here a regiment of Cantey's southern infantry, supported by artillery, opened fire suddenly on Veatch's closely massed column. Dodge, informed that Veatch's skirmishers had reported sighting the railroad, ordered one of the two advancing brigades to charge the Confederates, while the other brigade swung a little to the north to gain the cover of some low hills and timber and press forward to the railroad. Before these orders could be executed, however, Dodge received instructions from McPherson to recross the creek and return to the vicinity of Bald Hill.[16] No explanation for this order was given at the time or later, and no further effort to reach the railroad was made that afternoon. With the coming of darkness, McPherson ordered the Army of the

Tennessee to abandon the attempt to cut the railroad and issued orders instead to return to Snake Creek Gap and bivouac.[17] The disappointments on May 9 would not soon be forgotten.

CHAPTER 3

The Battle at the Angle

Despite the frustrations generated by McPherson's cautiousness, Sherman struggled to salvage what he could of the plan to force Joe Johnston to fight at Resaca. On the evening of May 11, orders were issued for all units to converge on Resaca. The Union army was to march before dawn the next morning via Villanow and Snake Creek Gap,[1] with only Oliver Howard's 4th Corps of the Army of the Cumberland following Johnston's retreating Confederates on the direct route from Dalton via the railroad to Resaca.[18] Three days rations and sixty rounds of ammunition were issued each man. The rapid march required that all unnecessary baggage be left behind, with only one wagon allowed for each regiment,

> Each man carried half his house on his back, a piece of heavy twilled muslin two yards square, with double rows of buttons and button-holes. His mate carried another similar piece, and the two, buttoned together and stretched between sticks, made shelter for the two. A canteen carried water or coffee, that he boiled for himself in a tin cup, or an old tomato can. A tin plate served as frying pan and serving dish. A green stick split at one end and forced over the rim of the plate made a handle to hold it over the fire, sometimes: at other times, the plate would lose its balance and into the fire would go the pork or hard tack.[19]

Since much of the march was at night over poorly marked roads, men with flaming torches were stationed at intervals along the route, while by day the passing columns were guided by boards nailed to trees as finger-posts.[20] Despite such precautions, delays were encountered as wagon trains blocked the narrow roads making detours necessary.[21]

By the afternoon of May 13, the arriving Federal units began to take their places near Resaca along the range of rugged, wooded hills that lined the western side of the narrow valley skirting Camp Creek and its tributaries. McPherson's army reoccupied Bald Hill, extending its right flank to the Oostanaula River thus covering the direct road from Snake Creek Gap to Resaca. Thomas' army, except for Oliver O. Howard's corps, was next on McPherson's left. Arriving on the morning of May 14, the Army of the Ohio, commanded by James Schofield, was ordered to extend the line northward along the creek. It was nearly 10 A.M. before all were ready to press toward the Confederate positions east of the intervening creek and valley.

Hearing that Howard's 4th Corps was approaching Resaca along the railroad from the north, driving the Confederate rear guard before it, Sherman ordered Thomas and Schofield to pivot from a point near Dodge's left on Bald Hill and swing north and east like a great closing door toward Camp Creek and the hills and railroad beyond. Henry Judah and Jacob Cox commanded the two divisions of the Army of the Ohio that took part in this movement, constituting the outer edge of this arch. It was the Union soldiers under Cox and Judah who bore the brunt of the Federal attack on the entrenched Confederate line at Camp Creek, May 14, 1864.

Jacob Cox, untrained in military arts, was a state senator in Ohio when the war came. Because of his political associations, he was able to secure appointment to high military rank in the first flurry of excitement in the days following Fort Sumter. Detailed to training duties at recruit centers around the state, he soon proved himself a capable and resourceful administrator. Cox became a serious student of the military profession, participating creditably under George B. McCellan in West Virginia. His dedication to duty and his political prominence were ultimately rewarded by the assignment to command a division of the Army of the Ohio during the Atlanta Campaign. Despite his lack of formal military training and distinguishing daring in battle, he nevertheless won the respect of Sherman who considered him courageous and reliable. At Resaca on May 14, Cox would have need to draw upon this reservoir of character.

At the time the movement toward Camp Creek began that day, Cox's division was on the west bank of the stream facing northeast. At

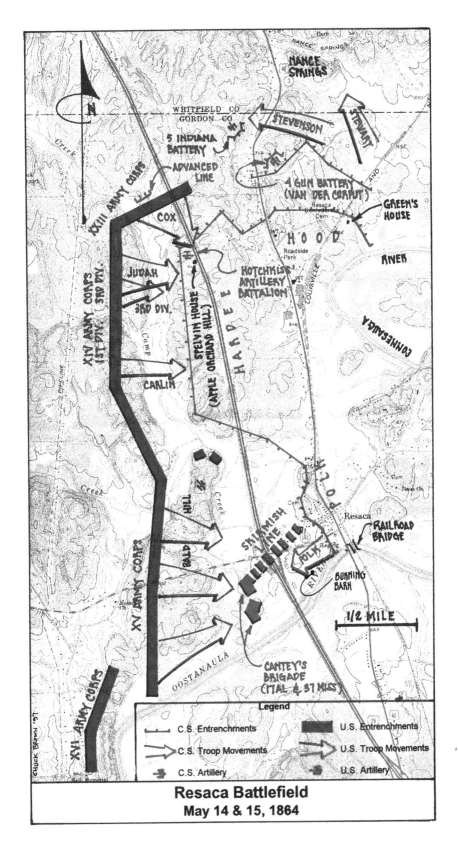

Resaca Battlefield
May 14 & 15, 1864

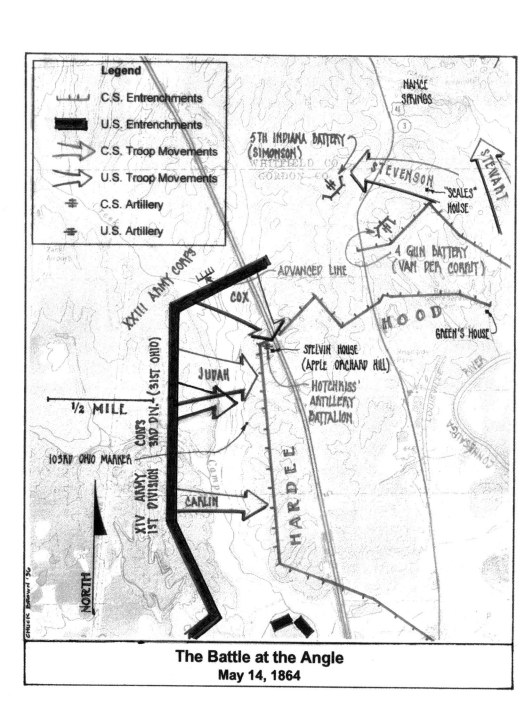

Legend

⊥⊥⊥	C.S. Entrenchments
▬▬▬	U.S. Entrenchments
⟹	C.S. Troop Movements
⟹	U.S. Troop Movements
⊧	C.S. Artillery
⊧	U.S. Artillery

NANCE SPRINGS

41

5TH INDIANA BATTERY (SIMONSON)

WHITFIELD CO.
GORDON CO.

STEVENSON

STEWART

"SCALES" HOUSE

4 GUN BATTERY (VAN DER CORPUT)

XXIII ARMY CORPS

ADVANCED LINE

COX

SPELVIN HOUSE (APPLE ORCHARD HILL)

HOOD

GREEN'S HOUSE

JUDAH

HOTCHKISS' ARTILLERY BATTALION

1/2 MILE

3RD DIV.- (31ST OHIO)

103RD OHIO MARKER

CORPS

HARDEE

XIV ARMY 1ST DIVISION

CARLIN

NORTH

CHUCK BROWN '96

The Battle at the Angle
May 14, 1864

the point where his division was located, the upper course of the creek makes an angle to the northwest, with a small branch coming into it from the northeast. The hills here are especially precipitous, running generally north to south and crowding the west bank of the stream. The terrain at this point is dominated by a series of razorback ridges bordering the western edge of the valley. Here, where the divisions of Cox and Judah approached the creek, the valley is less than 400 yards wide. The openness of the valley, one fork of which veers off somewhat to the northeast, enabled the Confederate batteries to deliver a flanking and frontal fire that swept the valley north and south. (See Map #5).

The first Federal unit to test this line of defense however, was William P. Carlin's brigade of the 1st Division of John M. Palmer's 14th Corps (Army of the Cumberland). Palmer had instructed his commanders that the march order of the day was a 130 degree pivot by the 14th, 23rd, and 4th corps marching east-northeast seeking the exact location of the Confederate defenses, yet keeping the right firmly anchored to the balance of the Cumberland army and McPherson's Army of the Tennessee at Bald Hill. Thus promptly at 9 A.M. on May 14, like a great swinging door, the movement began.

Carlin's brigade, being the extreme right, almost instantly made contact with the enemy. From Carlin's position on the bluff overlooking Camp Creek, he could view the valley beyond, and could see clearly the Confederate main line of defense 400 yards away on the corresponding ridge on the east side of the valley. By 11:30 A.M. the wheeling march of just over a mile brought the balance of the division abreast of Carlin and the assault began.

> General Carlin, who lay very near the creek mentioned, threw forward his skirmishers, driving those of the enemy within their works, and moved forward his lines across the creek. No sooner had his first line emerged from the woods than the enemy—infantry and artillery—opened upon it with terrible effect. Notwithstanding this, however, Carlin pushed forward both lines beyond the creek and nearly half way across the open field. The passage of the creek had, however, sadly disordered his lines, and finding it impossible to reform them while advancing so rapidly as the emergency of occasion required, hopeless, moreover of holding his position even if the

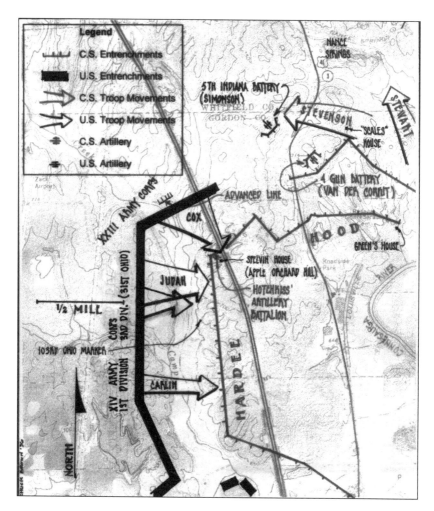

Map #5
The Battle at the Angle
May 14, 1864

assault should succeed, Carlin fell back to the cover of the creek, the
eastern bank of which offered in some places all the protection of a
well-constructed fortification.[22]

Here Carlin remained all day, keeping up a desultory fire against the
Confederate main line of defense on the east side of the valley. This
half-hearted and uncoordinated assault had cost the brigade 200
casualties. The brunt of the attack would be at the forks of the creek
this day some 400 yards to the left of Carlin's position, and would be
borne by the divisions of Cox and Judah.

Because of the greater distance to be covered and the more rugged
terrain encountered by Cox, Judah's division was the first unit of the
Army of the Ohio to strike the valley. Without waiting for Cox to
come up on his left, Judah made his attack. And it was here that the
great blunder of the day took place. As the Federal infantry units of
the 23rd Army Corps swung into place near the final ridge fronting
on the Confederate line at Camp Creek it was found that Milo
Hascall's brigade of Judah's division (23rd Army Corps) overlapped
John Turchin's brigade of the 3rd Division of the 14th Army Corps.
Here at the crucial point in the attack the two adjoining corps' flanks
were hopelessly intermingled resulting in command confusion.
Colonel M. B. Walker, 31st Ohio Volunteers (1st Brigade, 3rd
Division, 14th Army Corps) describes what happened next:

> Shortly after the brigade had arrived at the top of the hill it was
> observed that General Hascal's brigade of General Judah's division,
> was moving in a double line of battle to the front, on a line of direc-
> tion which brought it upon the rear of this brigade. Not
> understanding the nature of the movement, our lines stood fast
> until General Hascall's front line had passed our front line and his
> rear line our rear line. (See following drawing). Also see drawing,
> *Official Records,* Vol. 38, pt. 1, p.758):

(Hascall's first line)	Front Line
(Walker's first line)	Second Line
(Hascall's second line)	Third Line
(Walker's second line)	Fourth Line

At this time [Absalom] General Baird (14th Army Corps) gave the order that this brigade should advance as General Hascall's brigade (23rd Army Corps) advanced, and the troops were immediately ordered forward, advancing in the order they had assumed. The face of the country was very rough, rising and falling in a succession of high hills and deep gorges, covered with an almost impenetrably dense growth of timber, rendering it a very difficult matter for troops to advance in line. On reaching the second line of hills we passed our skirmish line, and were struck by the enemy's fire from their line, which had evidently been strengthened into a formidable line. The enemy also opened a heavy fire from artillery. Our lines steadily advanced, driving back the enemy, until we reached the crest of the last line of hills (overlooking the principal valley at Camp Creek), from which, for the first time, we gained a view of the enemy's entrenched lines. Our advance was here to some extent checked, some of the men in the lines stopping and lying down behind the crests of the hills, but the main portion of the lines rushed down the hill and charged toward the enemy's works, under a most murderous fire of canister and shell from the enemy's batteries, as well as the musketry from their lines. Our lines suddenly found themselves confronted by a deep, narrow stream, with quicksand in places, and steep muddy banks. The enemy's sharpshooters were posted here, but fled precipitately back to their works before our men. *No assaulting column had been formed* [italics added]. The creek proved a bar to our advance. Our troops sprang into the creek and opened fire on the rebel lines, then within seventy-five to one hundred yards of the enemy's works. It then appearing that our troops had fallen back from the hills, and the number of men who had gained the protection from the creek and remained there being very small and very much exposed, Col. M. B. Walker, being the ranking officer of the brigade present at the creek, ordered the men to fall back in single file, covering themselves the best way they could from the enemy's fire, at the same time keeping up as rapid fire as possible from the creek, and making it difficult for the enemy to use his artillery, except for one battery, or to fire from his lines. (*Official Records,* Vol 38, pt.1, p.759). [See also Map #5]

Thus in this manner Judah's attack was beaten back with heavy losses and forced to seek shelter behind the banks of the creek in the valley. For this fiasco General Judah was relieved of his command a few days later.

Meanwhile, before descending abruptly into the narrow valley, the brigades of Cox's division had been advancing in two lines without adequate artillery preparation or infantry support and had passed several steep ridges and ravines. Coming into the valley a few moments later, Cox advanced across the west fork of the creek without pausing to reconnoiter the terrain ahead. Crossing the creek, the regiments swept over some advanced works of Confederate General William J. Hardee's entrenched line. Hardee's outnumbered defenders fled across the small branch and valley behind them to the safety of the main line of defense on the high hills bordering the eastern side of the valley. The low hills won here in the fork of Camp Creek offered only partial protection for the brigades of Cox's division. It soon became apparent to Cox that with Judah's division on the right pinned down and helpless:

> Our flank was exposed to a galling artillery fire, as the ridge on which we were had its shoulder bare when it came into the valley, whose curve gave the enemy an enfilading fire upon us. His infantry sought also to drive us out of the position we had captured, and the fighting was heavy for an hour or two. But Howard's corps came up on our left, and we made firm our hold on the hills we had gained,

Maj. Gen. Jacob Dolson Cox led the 3rd Division, XXIII Corps at the Battle of Resaca. Unschooled in military science, Cox was an apt student, and quickly won the respect of General Sherman in the Atlanta Campaign. At Resaca, Cox's division was heavily engaged on May 14 at the Angle. After the war Cox became governor of Ohio and later Secretary of the Interior in Grant's administration.

Lt. General William J. Hardee, West Point graduate, famous author of *Rifle and Light Infantry Tactics*, better known as *Hardee's Tactics*. This manual of drill and tactics was used by soldiers on both sides. Veteran of the Mexican War, highly respected by all who knew him, and known to this soldiers as "Old Reliable", Hardee nevertheless seemed reluctant to accept offers of higher command, including command of the Army of Tennessee in the winter of 1863-64. At Resaca, Hardee's Corps occupied most of the line of defense at the Angle. Tragically, his 16 year old son was killed in one of the last battles of the war.

Picture #2
Sketch by Alfred R. Waud
Battle at the Angle
XXIII Army Corps & XIV Army Corps May 14, 1864

forcing the Confederates to adopt a new line curving to the eastward.[23]

Howard had witnessed the attack by Cox:

> It was the first time that my attention had been especially called to that handsome and gallant young officer and able man, Jacob D. Cox. He was following his troops, and appeared full of spirit and energy as he rode past the group of officers who were with us.[24]

During the height of the battle here at the angle in the Confederate line, Cox had a close brush with death. Standing with other officers at the edge of the woods near the position just won, a shell exploded among them. While Cox was uninjured, the concussion stunned Mahlon Manson, a brigade commander.

> Manson's experience was a curious illustration of the effect of such an accident. He was unaware of his hurt, and only thought, in the moment of failing consciousness as he fell, that the motion was that of his companions flying upward instead of his own falling: and on coming to himself in the hospital began to speak his sorrow for what he supposed was the death of his friends.[25]

Cox's division suffered 562 casualties in the attack. He had not been told that an assault was to be made on an entrenched position, and he, Carlin, and Judah had failed to coordinate their movements. All things considered, the limited success of Sherman's brigadiers at the forks of the creek that day was not especially surprising.

Across the valley, Hardee's Confederates had been allowed ample time to prepare. For two days they had been moving into position on the hills facing Judah and Cox. Hardee's corps had extended Polk's line northwest, with William Bate's division anchoring Hardee's right flank on the crest of a high hill overlooking the creek at the point where Cox made his attack. Major T. R. Hotchkiss's battalion of artillery occupied the hill immediately on Bate's right. To the left of Bate's, the veteran division of Patrick Cleburne completed its defensive preparations.

On the morning that Cox and Judah attacked, Confederate General John Bell Hood sent his corps into place, extending from

Hardee's right eastward across the main wagon road, the railroad, and beyond to the Conasauga River.[26] Where the entrenched lines of Hood and Hardee joined at the hill overlooking Camp Creek, a portion of Bate's division occupied an apple orchard near a white frame house. Here on a site preserved so well for history by the photographic art of Civil War cameraman George Barnard, the Kentucky brigade commanded by Colonel Joseph Lewis constructed their earthworks:

> The Kentuckians were on a bald hill where there was a frame house with a few apple trees about the yard and some rifle pits thrown up, and a battery of four guns, with a single line of infantry behind it. The Yankee lines, two deep, and double line of skirmishers (were) about 400 yards away across a ravine and a field and posted in a skirt of heavy timber on a ridge. They opened on the brave Kentuckians with about twenty pieces of artillery, and in a few minutes the two lines of skirmishers and the two lines of battle started with a rush across the open space; but they recoiled before they had gotten within a hundred yards of the Kentuckians, and as they retreated, the Yankee artillery opened again and cut down all four of our guns, then three lines of Yankee infantry returned to the assault. Onward they came; the gallant Kentuckians were standing to their work like men; but were about to be overpowered, when [Robert C.] Tyler's Brigade, that was lying over behind the hill, was ordered to their support; and when Tyler reached the Kentuckians line, the second repulse was complete in ten minutes.[27]

A little south of this point in Cleburne's front, a Federal officer was heard to address his troops encouraging them to renew the attack. He told them that they were the men who had taken Missionary Ridge, and they could take this. His eloquence availed little, however, for his man took but a few paces into the open ground in the valley, then retired quickly under the Confederate fire.[28] (See sketch of Battle at the Angle by A. R. Waud, Picture #2, next page)

After the repulse, the Federal artillery opened with what one member of Tyler's 20th Tennessee Regiment termed the "most terrific artillery fire I was under in the war."[29] The storm of shot and shell lasted almost three hours without slackening. A shell fell into a rifle pit in Tyler's line, where it lay sizzing and ready to explode. Lieut. F. M. Clark and A. H. Lankford each grabbed at it and together threw it out of the works. It exploded before it struck the ground. The works were strengthened on the night of the 14th.[30]

Hotchkiss' battery on the brow of the hill at the angle where Hardee's and Hood's lines joined was a special target for the Federal gunners. The Union artillery had occupied a long wooded ridge directly across the valley at a distance of less than 500 yards. Despite the heavy traverses constructed by the Confederates on the hill, and the work of Cleburne's elite band of sharpshooters equipped with the fine Whitworth sniper rifles, two of Hotchkiss' guns were disabled, and a second battery nearby received heavy damage to three of its guns. Lieutenant W.P. Wiygle of the 24th Mississippi became so distraught at the death of six men and the wounding of five others from his company by the explosion of a single shell that he fled from the field.

Among those contributing to the havoc of Hardee's line was Captain Hubert "Leather Britches" Dilger of the Battery I, Ohio Light Artillery. Dilger's famous battery and the other nearby batteries were so effective that by 11 A.M. on May 15 Hotchkiss' battery was silenced, and in some places the nearby infantry breastworks and traverses were almost obliterated by the terrific storm of incoming shells.[31]

Picture #3
Captain Hubert "Leather Britches" Dilger, Battery I
1st Ohio Light Artillery

Photo #4a
A collection of scenes of the fields of Battle at the Angle. (4a-4e)
Battlefield at the Angle looking eastward across Camp Creek valley toward
Confederate entrenchments on ridge. Note grave markers in foreground in this
1864 photograph. Camera position apparently at foot of ridge occupied by XIV and
XXII army corps. Hitherto unpublished photo.

Picture #4b

This 1864 photograph from the ridge overlooking the battle valley at Camp Creek is focused on a small white frame house by a small apple orchard near the point of junction of Hood's and Hardee's corps. See details of the fight at this point by Confederate Colonel Joseph Lewis' Kentucky brigade, p. 25. Note the cannonball on the ground in foreground.

Picture #4c

In this view of the apple orchard and nearby white frame house the camera position has been shifted a short distance to the right of the previous location. Note the artillery-shattered tree in foreground. The white frame house is believed to be the Spelvin House. When Interstate 75 was cut through this ridge near the house site in 1960, a dug well was discovered.

Picture #4d
In this photograph by George Barnard in 1864, the camera position has been shifted across the Camp Creek valley to a point on the ridge occupied by Hardee's Confederate Corps. In the foreground are shattered trees and confederate earthworks, and in the middle distance the white frame house shown in the previous scenes. This view is looking generally north.

Picture #4e
Same camera position as in the previous photograph. This time however, a person believed to be the photographer George Barnard is seated on the stump in the foreground.

CHAPTER 4

Stopped by the 5th Indiana Battery

By mid-afternoon on May 14, Sherman abandoned the attempt to carry the defenses at the Confederate angle near Camp Creek. Farther north and over to the east near the Dalton-Resaca wagon road, elements of Howard's 4th Corps began to arrive from their march down the railroad from Dalton. Driving Joe Wheeler's cavalry and a brigade of Hood's infantry before them, they took position on Cox's left flank. Brigadier General John Newton's division of the 4th Corps replaced the exhausted men of Cox's force, allowing Cox to retire to the rear where his men rested and replenished their ammunition. Thomas J. Wood's division of the 4th Corps moved up on Newton's left, occupying a ridge overlooking the wagon road to Resaca. General William B. Hazen's brigade of Wood's division was warmly engaged as it succeeded in fortifying a hill that overlooked the small valley. (See Map #6).

As the third division of Howard's corps commanded by General David S. Stanley arrived from Dalton, forcing the last of Johnston's rear guard down the railroad, Sherman discovered that the distance between Wood's left and the river (Conasauga) was too great for Stanley's forces to cover. The Confederates quickly detected this flaw in the Federal alignment, and Hood was ordered to attack. The divisions commanded by Carter Stevenson and A.P. Stewart were chosen for the task, but it was almost 5 P.M. before the movement got underway. Stewart's men constituted the extreme right of the Confederate line with the left connecting with Stevenson near the Resaca-Dalton wagon road. Stevenson's regiments on the crest of the ridge east of the wagon road served as the pivot in what was planned as a great wheeling movement toward the exposed Federal flank and rear. Although the Confederate divisions began the advance almost simultaneously, Stewart's men, having the greater distance to cover, did not succeed in

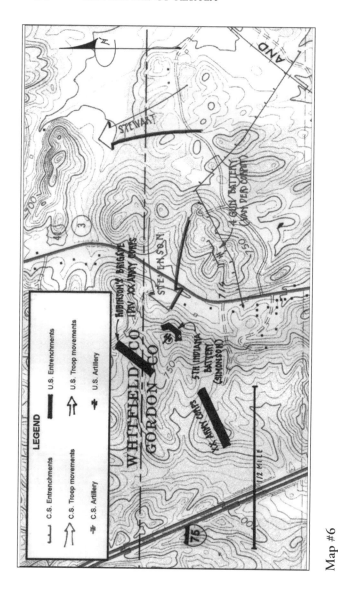

Map #6

Fight at the Fifth Indiana Battery Afternoon, May 14, 1864

Confederate attacks by Stevenson's and Stewart's divisions late afternoon May 14, 1864. Attack repulsed by the 5th Indiana Battery and the arrival of Federal reinforcements.

making contact with the enemy. Disorganized by rough terrain and some long-range artillery fire, Stewart halted his division after fifteen or twenty minutes to reorganize his straggling lines, but darkness intervened before the advance could be resumed.

Meanwhile, Stevenson's two brigades, having the shorter distance to cover, made contact with Sherman's exposed flank almost immediately. Those Federal regiments constituting the extreme left of the Union line just east of the wagon road received the brunt of Stevenson's attack. From their concealment on these hilltops many Union soldiers could see the Confederates forming in two lines, as though on dress parade with flags floating in the evening breeze. Many Confederate officers were mounted, and the light line of cavalry that protected the rear and flanks of the assaulting column could be seen clearly. The Union skirmishers were hurriedly reinforced but most of these were captured in the first Confederate rush. The attack struck first at Stanley's right brigade and broke it. One of the advanced units nearby was the 96th Illinois Regiment—it could see little from where it was but it heard everything, and in a moment it too was struck by the storm of advancing Confederate infantry:

> Rebs could be plainly heard as they threw aside a fence in front. Most of us were generally kneeling or lying prostrate. Colonel [Thomas E.] Champion: "Steady men! Hold your fire until I give the word!" Not until the bushes began to wave to and fro in our very faces did we get the order to Fire![32]

Great confusion then followed, and in it Colonel Champion's order to retreat was not heard. "Rebels were past both flanks, and yelling and firing with all their might."[33] There was utter confusion among the men of the 96th Illinois and the other nearby Federal regiments. In wild disorder, a race between men in blue and men in gray began. The flight took Stanley's regiments through a depression where the pines served as a cover and screen. Mounting the hill west of the wagon road, the fleeing regiments passed to the left of Captain Peter Simonson's 5th Indiana Battery which was in position atop the hill. A frantic effort was made here to rally the panic-stricken regiments to protect the Federal battery. There was a momentary lull in the fighting; then on came Carter Stevenson's two Confederate brigades directly at the battery. It was

> marvelous to witness the rapidity with which the artillery was fired as the danger of capture became apparent to the cannoneers. Perhaps never were six guns made to do more rapid and destructive work. They were filled again and again, almost to the muzzle, and fired so rapidly the Rebel prisoners captured soon afterward refused to believe that but a single battery had played upon them.[3] (See sketch, Figure 12a, *Harper's Weekly*).

The attacking rebels soon directed most of their attention at the battery. A column stealthily approached the guns from the flank with orders not to return the fire of the Union infantry but to concentrate every effort to overpower the gunners with bayonets. The Confederates were within a few rods of the battery when a brigade from the 20th Corps arrived on the scene and took its place beside the guns.[2] In a few moments the Confederate ranks were shattered and routed from the field. Numerous prisoners were taken, and the ground was strewn with arms and equipment. Most of the dead and wounded were abandoned on the field by Stevenson's gallant but out-manned Confederates.[35] Since only two brigades of Carter Stevenson's division and the three brigades under A. P. Stewart were available for the task, the effort was too feeble to pose a decisive threat. Nevertheless, Sherman's left was saved from serious damage that day by the combination of a poorly coordinated Confederate attack, the coming of nightfall, and a generous measure of good luck.

Note: This was Robinson's Brigade (Col. James S. Robinson, 3rd. Brigade, 1st. Division, 20th Corps). Robinson describes the rescue of the 5th Indiana Battery:

> by 6:30 p.m. the head of my column reached a high wooded ridge, overlooking a narrow open valley, along which extended the main road leading to dalton. on the farther side of the valley was another thickly wooded hill, and upon a slight knoll in the open field at our feet stood the Fifth Indiana Battery, supported by a por-tion of Stanley's division....it was evident that General Stanley's lines were falling back; in fact they were giving away in some disorder.

arriving at the front of the battery the eighty-second illinois, sixty-first ohio, and one hundred and forty-third new york volunteers poured a tremendous fire upon the overconfident foe. meeting with such severe and unexpected resistance, the enemy at once gave way and confusedly sought his entrenchments back in the woods. (official records, vol. 38, pt.2, pp. 85-86).

Also, see Figure 5a, following page. (From *Harper's Weekly*, June 28, 1864). Sketch highly inaccurate.

Harper's Weekly

Picture #5
The campaign in Georgia–Robinson's Brigade, of Hooker's corps, saving the Fifth Indiana battery, May 14, 1864.

CHAPTER 5

Polk's Battlefield

A lmost at the same time the fight for Simonson's battery was taking
place north of the village, a struggle was in progress for some key
hills east of Camp Creek on the extreme Union right. It was on these
hills that Sherman's opportunity to trap and crush the Confederate
army at Resaca passed unnoticed. (See Map#7).

The decision to capture these hills seems, in retrospect, to have
been almost an afterthought. The bald hills west of the creek had been
occupied by McPherson's 15th and 16th corps on May 13. Here
artillery was placed, and a long-range fire from the entrenched guns
was maintained on the railroad bridge spanning the Oostanaula less
than three quarters of a mile away.[36] By the morning of May 14, skirmishers of the 15th Corps had been advanced into the valley to the
creekline, the banks of which provided a degree of cover and concealment from rifle musket and artillery fire. The sound of battle north of
town on the Federal left flank late in the day prompted McPherson to
order an assault on the group of low hills east of the creek. Two
brigades of Logan's corps were assigned the task of driving Polk's
Confederates from these hills. Whatever the outcome, McPherson
counted on the effort preventing Polk from sending aid to the
Confederates attacking Sherman's left.[37]

It was almost 6 P.M. before Logan was ready. At a bugle signal the
Union artillery ceased firing, and the nine attacking regiments leaped
from the protection of the creek bank and rushed into the field toward
the enemy's position on the hills less than fifty yards away. The field
was full of logs and briars, and a muddy slough had to be waded
almost at the start. Overcoming these obstacles, and with colors flying
they

> nobly dashed through a hail-storm of lead and iron, which
> belched forth from the enemy's batteries and riflepits. Reaching the

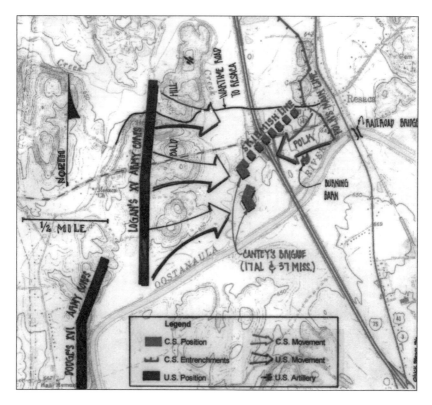

Map #7
Polk's Battlefield, May 14, 1864 (6 to 10 PM)
Polk's main battle line followed the small hills just west of the railroad bridge at the
river and the village of Resaca, to a hilltop point just north of town (a small
cemetary is located on this site today). Then the line followed some low hills north-
westwardly to a higher hill where Polk's right flank tied in to Hardee's Confederate
corps overlooking Camp Creek at the creek valley (See 1864 photograph of Polk's
battlefield from this point). The heaviest fighting on Polk's front was near the south
end of the battle line where two understrength Confederate regiments were driven
from their advanced position on some hills overlooking Camp Creek. Polk's efforts
to retake these hills were unsuccessful.

base of the hill, they climbed the slope, and, running over the crest of the first undulation in the eminence, fairly effected a lodgment, under cover of a dip in the plateau. The hurrah of thousands of admiring friends followed the onward march of this command.[38]

Cantey's small Confederate brigade was quickly swept from its crude rifle pits and breastworks of logs by this impetuous rush. The raw recruits of the 17th Alabama and the 37th Mississippi regiments of this brigade had been roughly handled a few days before in the defense of Resaca on May 9. On May 14, Cantey's brigade was not only poorly supported, it was psychologically unprepared for the task assigned it. Later a Confederate officer remembered that

> There were some brave spirits in both regiments who continued to pour it into the enemy from behind trees while the Federals occupied the crest of the ridge. We stopped all the men we could and put them in our line. I said to one fellow:"Halt! What are you running for?" He answered, "Bekase I kain't fly!"[39]

From the main Confederate line 400 yards away, near the town, a destructive pointblank fire poured into the newly-won Union position. The artillery directed at Logan's men became one continuous roar, with shells bursting over and in the Federal ranks.[40] After a half hour of shelling, the Confederate fire slackened, giving the attackers an opportunity to entrench. Reinforcements were hurried across the creek during the respite, and these quickly extended the Federal line to the Oostanaula River. Only fifty yards away, under cover of another round-top hill, the survivors of Cantey's shattered brigade were rapidly being reinforced. Too late Polk realized that the possession of the hills just captured would enable Federal artillery to bring the railroad bridge under fire at a range of little more than a quarter of a mile. The hills must be regained at whatever cost!

The Union commanders were just as determined to defend their newly-won advantage. As many men as could be spared were taken from the firing line to aid the pioneers (military engineer units) in strengthening the log works for the attack all knew would soon come. Skirmishers were advanced as far as possible, and flank defenses were occupied.

These dispositions were scarcely made when our skirmishers were driven in, followed closely by the enemy, who had massed a large force in our front, and seemed determined to retake the position at all hazards. Colonel [Americus V.] Rice, Fifty-seventh Ohio, in whose immediate front they were advancing in column by regiments, opened a murderous fire by rank, and with deadly effect. Lieutenant-Colonel [Frank S.] Curtis, One hundred and twenty-seventh Illinois, stationed on Colonel Rice's right, opened a cross-fire on the same column; other portions of the line on the left also delivered a well-directed fire on their right flank, notwithstanding which they advanced to within thirty yards of our line before they were checked, and then only falling back to reform and renew the attack, threatening my right flank. They were again repulsed, and again rallied for another onset.[41]

Reinforced, Cantey's column, badly outnumbered, advanced during a lull to the ravine just below the ridge occupied by the Federals. Leaving their canteens behind so as to reduce the noise of their approach, and partially concealed by the lateness of the hour and the smoke of the battlefield, they stealthily took their positions in the ravine near the unsuspecting Federal soldiers. They could see the blue line under the smoke on the crest of the ridge. The order was given:

Ready! Aim! Fire! Fifteen hundred rifles belched forth, fired as one man. Then there was a tremendous confusion among the enemy—calling for litterbearers and their officers rallying the men, who had fallen back behind the crest of the ridge.[42]

Union reinforcements were called for quickly, and soon fresh regiments were crossing the creek "at the double-quick and a cheer." Another attack by the Confederates was repulsed. By 8 P.M. Polk abandoned the effort to retake the hills. The sounds of battle continued, however, until nearly 10 P.M., the field partially illuminated by the flames of a burning barn nearby. Stubborn pockets of Cantey's and Loring's men continued to fire into the darkness toward the prized hills from which they had been driven.[43]

While Sherman failed to fully grasp the tactical significance of this success by McPherson on the evening of May 14, the loss of these hills so near Johnston's line of retreat was to prove decisive. Johnston could see that should Sherman choose to attack Polk in force, disaster for the Confederates was likely. Strangely, although Sherman felt confident of "bagging all the rebels in Resaca," he seemed preoccupied with preparing defenses should Polk choose to attack, and with maintaining supplies for a rapid march should the Confederates choose to escape rather than fight.[44] Except for the division guarding the river crossings near Calhoun, Johnston had every available man in the line at Resaca. There was no reserve with which to block a breakthrough. He knew that, at the very least, Union artilley on those hills would make the village and railroad untenable. Like General Robert E. Lee at Sharpsburg [Antietam], Johnston had a deep river at his back and was without a reserve. As at Sharpsburg, the Union commander had corps-size reserves, yet dared not use them.

The position won here on the evening of May 14, placed Sherman's right less than 500 yards from the railroad and only a little farther from the pontoon foot bridges over which the Confederates were to escape the following night. To an alert and aggressive commander, the half-mile wide corridor of gentle hills spanning Sherman's front from the river on the right to the nearest ridge on his left would have suggested an opportunity to carry the fight to his opponent. With only Polk's newly-constituted and un-battle tested corps between him and almost certain destruction of the Confederate army, Sherman chose instead to spend the next day entrenching artillery on the newly-won hills.

Picture #6a

Collection of wartime views (scenes) of the fields of battle on Polk's Battlefield

Hardee's entrenchments looking south across Polk's battlefield toward the Oostenaula River. Polk's right flank tied in to Hardee's line near this point. Note the artillery positions nearby facing to the right toward Camp Creek valley, and see in the distance what appears to be a military wagon train parked facing the village (Resaca is to the left out of the picture). This is a previously unpublished 1864 photograph.

Picture #6b
Collection of wartime views (scenes) of the fields of battle on Polk's Battlefield
May 14, 1864
View in 1864 looking south toward Resaca village and railroad bridge (a covered bridge) over the Oostenaula River.

Picture #6c
Collection of wartime views (scenes) of the fields of battle on Polk's Battlefield
View in 1864 from Polk's battle line from the next hill north from the photograph shown on the previous page. This is the hill today that contains the small cemetary mentioned earlier. The hill and cemetary is owned by the city of Resaca. Remains of the entrenchments seen in this picture can be traced today.

CHAPTER 6

The Fight for the Four-Gun Battery

Even Joe Johnston appeared not to grasp fully the import of the loss of the hills in Polk's front, for he seemed more concerned about a force of enemy that had pushed across the Oostanaula some distance south of Resaca near Calhoun.(See Map#6).

> At 9 P.M. I...received from Major-General [William T.] Martin a report that Federal infantry was crossing the Oostanaula, near Calhoun on a pontoon bridge.[45]

Johnston did not learn until later that the force was but a portion of a single division from Dodge's 16th Corps. The crossing had been accomplished where Snake Creek empties into the river. While one brigade set up a noisy covering fire a short distance upstream near Lay's Ferry, six companies using pontoon boats had crossed the river at the creek. Before other units could exploit the success however, the small force was recalled to the west bank of the river when word was received (later proven unfounded) that a Confederate unit had crossed farther upstream and was threatening to isolate the Federal division.

It was dark before Johnston received news of this threat to his line of supplies. The division at Calhoun was dispatched to aid the Confederate cavalry at the threatened point. The orders for Hood to resume the attack on Howard at daybreak the next day were cancelled but were reissued again near noon when word was received that the news of the crossing near Lay's Ferry was "false." A brigade each from Polk and Hardee was selected to support the divisions of Stewart and Stevenson in the proposed attack on Howard's position on May 15.[46] (See Map#8).

It was nearly three P.M. on May 15 before Stewart and Stevenson received orders to renew the attack of the evening before on the

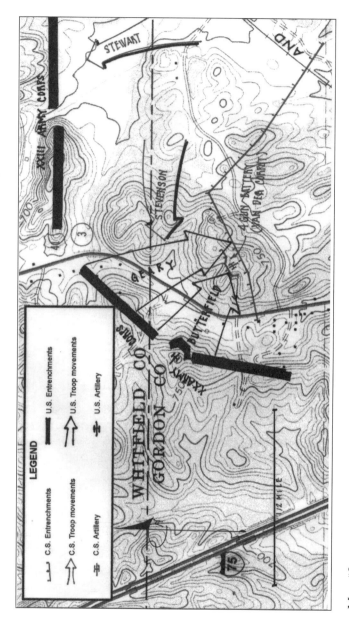

Map #8
Fight for the Four Gun Battery
3:00 PM to Midnight, May 15, 1864

Federal left. The advance was to depend upon the Federals' not having attacked first. Shortly before 4 P.M. Stewart learned of heavy enemy columns moving near his left front. There was a short delay while this information was relayed to Hood and Johnston. Receiving no reply, and assuming that the original orders to attack still stood, Stewart set his division in motion precisely at 4 P.M., advancing by wheeling to the left in conjunction with a similar movement by Stevenson. Hood's third division commanded by Thomas C. Hindman, was ordered to assist the attack but was unable to advance because of the proximity of enemy breastworks in its front. Thus Johnston's attack by "Hood's Corps" on May 15, was a repetition of the undermanned affair of the evening before—two divisions supported by two additional brigades, against two full corps.

The situation was further complicated when W. H. T. ["Shot Pouch"] Walker, commander of the Confederate division at Lay's Ferry, sent word to Johnston at noon that the "Federal right was crossing the river."[47] (See Map#9). Actually, only one of Dodge's divisions was involved in the successful crossing of the river near Calhoun. Since there is no indication that Sherman contemplated an immediate shift of his army to the right to exploit whatever advantage might be gained by the crossing, it seems reasonable to assume that Dodge's effort on May 15 was simply a reconaissance in force, designed to establish a bridgehead for possible future action should rapid pursuit of the Confederates be necessary.[48] By mid-afternoon the division was across the Oostanaula, entrenched, and in sufficient strength to beat off a weak attack by Walker's Southerners. After the initial repulse, Walker made no further effort to drive his opponent from this position. Learning of this enemy force in his rear, and misinterpreting it as a major shift of Sherman's army southward, Johnston revoked his orders to Hood to attack the Federal left north of Resaca. Hood was unable, however, to notify either Stevenson or Stewart in time to prevent the movement.

Bad judgment and poor communications continued to plague the Confederate offensive efforts. Carter Stevenson interpreted Hood's instructions to attack to mean that he should merely support Stewart's assault on the Union lines.[49] Also, contrary to what is generally believed, in this unsuccessful Confederate effort on May 15, neither

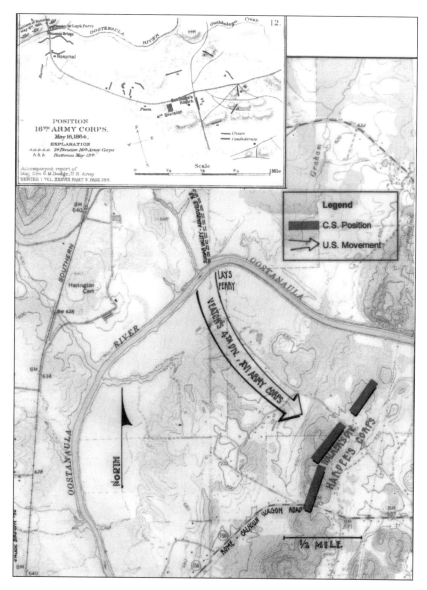

Map #9
The Lays Ferry battlefield south of Resaca.
May 14 & 15, 1864

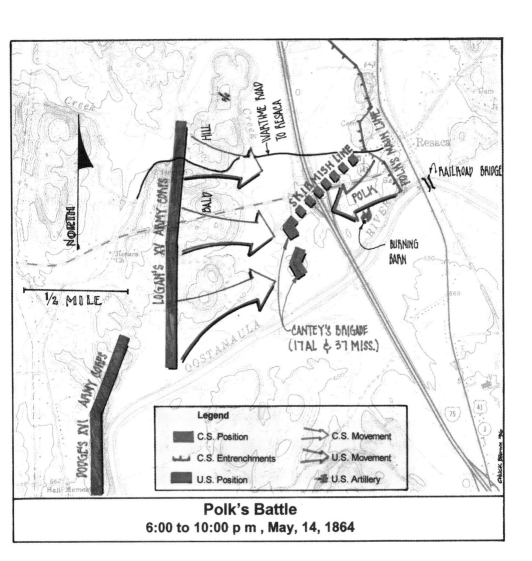

Polk's Battle
6:00 to 10:00 p m , May, 14, 1864

(Map labels:)

Creek

HILL

WARTIME ROAD TO RESACA

SKIRMISH LINE

POLK

POLK'S MAIN LINE

Resaca

RAILROAD BRIDGE

NORTH

LOGAN'S XV ARMY CORPS

BALD

RIVER

BURNING BARN

½ MILE

OOSTANAULA

CANTEY'S BRIGADE (17 AL & 37 MISS.)

DODGE'S XVI ARMY CORPS

Hall Memorial

CHUCK BROWN '96

Legend

C.S. Position
C.S. Entrenchments
U.S. Position

C.S. Movement
U.S. Movement
U.S. Artillery

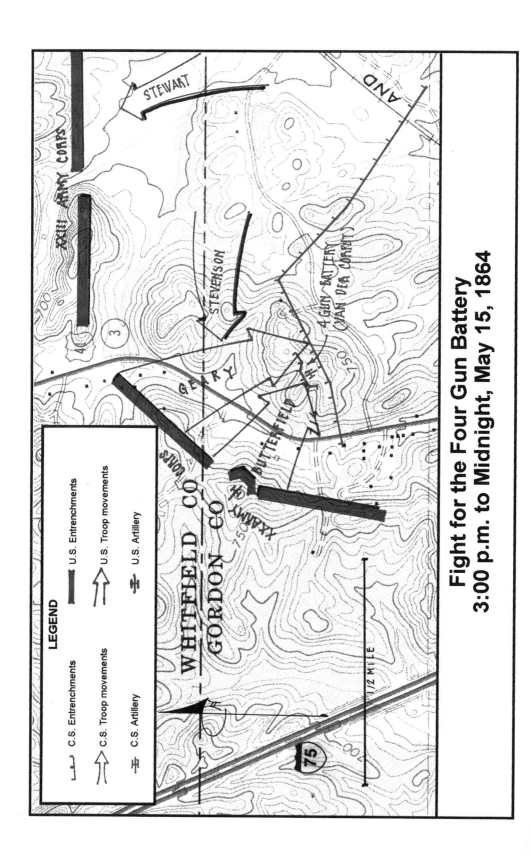

LEGEND

C.S. Entrenchments
U.S. Entrenchments
C.S. Troop movements
U.S. Troop movements
C.S. Artillery
U.S. Artillery

STEWART

XXIII ARMY CORPS

LAND

STEVENSON

4 GUN BATTERY
(VAN DEN CORPUT)

GEARY

BUTTERFIELD

XIV ARMY

WHITFIELD CO.
GORDON CO.

1/2 MILE

75

Fight for the Four Gun Battery
3:00 p.m. to Midnight, May 15, 1864

Stevenson nor Stewart received orders from Hood or Johnston countermanding the attack. Stevenson's brigades, cooperating with Stewart's wheeling columns, were already several hundred yards in advance of their trenches when they were stopped by a collision with the incoming waves of assaulting Federal forces bent upon an attack of their own. The Confederate attack was unsuccessful on May 15, not because Stevenson failed to support Stewart's advance as many have mistakenly supposed, but simply because the task required of Stewart and Stevenson was too great for the numbers assigned to it—five Confederate brigades assaulting two full Union corps.[50]

For the foot soldier in Stewart's and Stevenson's divisions, May 15 was a mix of confusion, frustration, and bloodshed. First Lieutenant T.P. Preston of the 42nd Alabama participated in the charge. He was severely wounded close to the Union breastworks. Taken prisoner, he was carried to a Federal field hospital. There a leg was amputated and the surgeon who attended him was considerate enough to write Preston's brother in Tennessee requesting money and clothing for the seriously wounded officer. Despite the care however, Preston died soon after the battle and was buried in a nearby trench.[51]

Another victim that day was Colonel A.R. Lankford of the 38th Alabama who seized the colors of his regiment and "bore them forward until he was captured by the enemy, they deeming him too brave to be shot."[52] The 13th New Jersey of Joe Hooker's 20th Corps was among the Federal units that witnessed the approach of the 38th Alabama. Pausing in their own attack near a peach orchard close to a frame building owned by John Scales, the New Jersey soldiers withheld their fire until the Confederates were within 120 yards—their volley left the field littered with dead and wounded from Stewart's gallant band.[53]

The Federal attack that stalled the advance of Stevenson's and Stewart's divisions was the work of Joe Hooker's 20th Corps of the Army of the Cumberland. Sherman, preoccupied with forcing the Confederates to constrict their lines north of the village while strangely ignoring the opportunity to seal off the Southern army's only avenue to escape at the other end of the line near the railroad bridge at the Oostanaula, ordered Hooker to plan an afternoon assault on the Confederate position east of the wagon road. Hooker was thorough in his preparation. Troop formations and routes of approach were discussed in detail with his division commanders. Time was permitted for unit commanders to make a field reconnaissance of the terrain in their front. Hooker's corps was to attack in column of brigades— "that is, each brigade in line, and one following another with no great intervals between them."[54] Howard's 4th Corps was to support the attack on the right, while the Army of the Ohio was to advance on Hooker's left. Howard's left would serve as the pivot for the eastward and southward moving Federal columns.[55] Hooker's immediate objectives were confined to driving in the outlying enemy fortified points and gaining assault positions in close proximity to the rebel breastworks. Carefully planned, and designed to achieve only limited objectives, it failed, nevertheless, in execution. The attack was disrupted by rugged hills, covered with briar and pine thickets, confused by an unexpected collision with advancing Confederate infantry, and finally stalled by the first major fort it encountered. Even Joe Hooker had enjoyed better days than this. (See Maps #10 and #11 "Blakeslee Maps").

The ground in front of Hooker's and Howard's corps was very rough, with stony knolls sparsely covered with trees. Hooker's corps moved from the ridge west of the Resaca wagon road, crossed the narrow valley, and climbed the hills bordering the road on the east. Colonel Benjamin Harrison, commanding the 70th Indiana Regiment of General Daniel Butterfield's division, found himself directly before a lunette containing a Confederate battery of four guns—"The fort being simply a natural basin on the ridge, with formidable breastworks flanking it on the right and left...."[56] This, Captain Max Van Den Corput's Cherokee Artillery, had occupied a salient point atop a thickly wooded hill fifty paces in front of Stevenson's main line of infantry. Before adequate measures could be taken to protect the battery, Stevenson received repeated and preemptory orders from Hood to open fire on a battery on the opposing ridge that was annoying Hindman's line. The Cherokee Artillery had hardly gotten into position before the Confederate skirmishers were driven in by Hooker's advancing lines of battle. The suddenness of the attack enabled Hooker's corps to secure a lodgment in a ravine below. The proximity

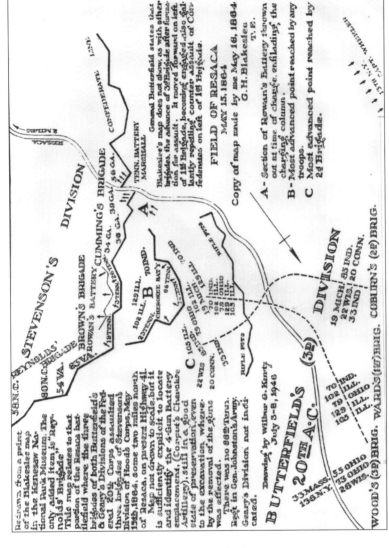

Map #10
Blakeslee/Kurtz Map
Artist/Historian Wilbur Kurtz made this copy of a print of the Blakeslee Map when it was located in the Kennesaw Battlefield Park museum in 1946. The Blakeslee Map was sketched by G.H. Blakeslee, a topographical engineer of the Federal 20th Corps on May 16, 1864, the day after the battle when the Federals were in possession of the field. This map (with Kurtz' notes) shows the troop positions and assault routes of two of Butterfield brigades in the attack on the Four Gun Battery on May 15, 1864.

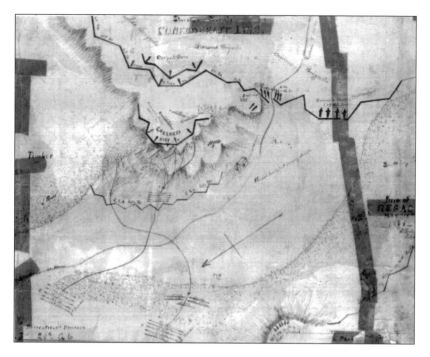

Map #11

Blakeslee/Corput Map

This map is believed to have been drawn by Captain Max Van Den Corput (commander of the Four Gun Battery at Resaca) or one of his brothers. However, "whoever drew this map had Blakeslee's map before him for it is substantially a duplicate of it. It is on the back of a portion of a gaudy lithograph advertising the festival of the Veiled Prophets in St. Louis, October 4 (year unknown)"– (Kurtz notes).

The major conflict between this map and the Blakeslee/Kurtz Map is the absence of Confederate infantry in the gun fort, and the position of Rowan's Confederate Battery during the battle. Captain Corput, rather than Blakeslee, is the better authority in each instance.

of the combatants isolated the battery so that while the Federals were unable to capture it, the Confederates were helpless to retrieve it without first driving off the enemy massed on the slopes and ravine in front.[57] (See Map 11#, also photo of Butterfield's trench Picture #9).

> So near the guns and beneath a crest were the men (Hooker's) that they by their fire almost paralyzed (the guns) use against our advancing lines. These guns, however, at intervals did bloody work, using canister and shells against brigades further off.[58]

Harrison's regiment had gained the outer face of the embrasure. After pausing a moment to catch their breath, they arose and rushed over the guns, "striking down and bayoneting the rebel gunners, many of whom defiantly stood by their guns till struck down."[59] The Confederates soon rallied and poured in a destructive fire that forced the Federals back to the outer face of the embrasure. At about this time, the attack by Stewart and Stevenson struck the center and left of Hooker's columns, increasing the confusion near the point of the four-gun battery. Adjustments were made, and the Confederates were driven back (one division of the Army of the Ohio assisting in this effort), but the momentum of the Federal attack was irretrievably lost (See Picture #7).

With the Federal attack stalled at most points, Corput's battery became the center of a holocaust produced by the simultaneously advancing and constantly reinforcing columns of blue and gray. Colors were planted near the guns time and again, then lost and recovered as the outcome of the bitterly fought contest for the guns remained in doubt. Sergeant Frederick Hess, color bearer for the 129th Illinois of Butterfield's division, chagrined to hear the shrill triumphant cry of the Confederates, at once unfurled his flag, swinging it toward them in defiance. He instantly fell, but other hands grasped the flag, and it came back only to return and wave from the very spot where its former bearer fell.[60]

Major Stephen Pierson of the 33rd New Jersey recalled later his experience in this action:

> It was an "old field" up which we went, grown up with young pines 10 or 12 feet high. The Major was sick, and I, as Adjutant,

was looking after the right wing of the Regiment by order of Lieut. Col. [Enos] Fourat, who commanded the Regiment during the rest of the campaign. The Rebel fire was a little high, and I can see now the little tops of those pine trees fall as the minie bullets cut them off just above the heads of the men who were advancing. We forced them back into the main line of works, but again they were too strong for us to carry by assault. But we hugged them tight, and by a steady and accurate fire cut off a battery of theirs which occupied a prominent salient, jutting out some distance from their main line. But we had gotten, and held on to, a position so close and advantageous that we were able to pick off and kill or wound every man who tried to load or fire the guns, and they finally gave up the attempt to use them. After dark we dug a hole through the side of the parapet near us and hauled two of the guns out. The Third Division of our Corps was on our left during this fight and assisted in the capture of the guns.[61] (See Blakeslee Map#11).

On the approach to the four-gun battery, Hooker's Third Division (Butterfield's) found it necessary to pass through portions of other regiments lying prone on the intervening hills. Members of the 96th Illinois, one of the regiments over which the advancing division had to stumble, had a clear view of a tragic fiasco that occured during the Federal assault:

Further over the ridge a terrible blunder occurred. Changing direction slightly, one column moved so as to partly come in rear of another, the woods so full of smoke they could not see what was before them, they fired into their friends.[62]

At dark the men of the Second and Third divisions united in their effort to secure the capture of the four-gun battery. Tools for digging and drag ropes were obtained:

As soon as night had fallen a strong detachment of ... determined men crept silently under the little fort and began removing the earth, logs, and stones of which it was constructed. Their work was overheard by the vigilant enemy, and a sharp engagement followed, which lighted up the whole crest of the hill; but while their comrades fought, these sappers and miners continued their work, and near midnight, when all was ready, a sudden dash was made, the drag ropes made fast, and with a burst of cheers and laughter the four guns were sent trundling down the hill to the rear of the Union lines.[63] (See sketch from *Harper's Weekly,* Picture #8).

Despite the rejoicing produced by the capture of the Confederate battery, it was quite clear to all that the Union gains that day had fallen far short of expectations. Hooker had handled his corps at Resaca no better than he had his army the year before at Chancellorsville.

Disturbed by erroneous reports of strong Federal columns crossing the river west of Calhoun, and apprehensive about the Union success in Polk's front the night before, Johnston, taking advantage of the escape route Sherman neglected to close, quietly and skillfully abandoned Resaca on the night of May 15. The trapped foe had slipped through Sherman's grasp to live to fight another day. Because the Confederates abandoned the field, the Union commander could claim victory at Resaca. But Sherman was surely aware that a great opportunity to destroy his foe and end the Atlanta Campaign then and there, had been lost. Here, close to his secure base of supplies at Chattanooga, with his foe trapped with back and flank to rivers, and with nearly a two-to-one advantage in numbers, Sherman chose not to "go in for the kill" as Grant would surely have done under similar circumstances. Rather, he remained relatively passive, ignoring Grant's earlier instructions to "move against Johnston's army, to break it up." Sherman's opportunity to "break up" Johnston's army was perfectly set on May 15 after Logan's successes the evening before on Polk's front. Using McPherson's entire army, augmented with nearby portions of Thomas' huge Army of the Cumberland, and with the right flank of this assaulting column safely anchored on the Oostanaula River, Polk's understrength and inexperienced corps would have been overwhelmed, and the railroad and foot bridge captured. Pinned in a pocket with his back to a river and cut off from his railroad supply line, Johnston's army would most certainly have been doomed. With the Confederate opponent destroyed, the Atlanta Campaign would have ended with Resaca, and Sherman would have been free to accomplish virtually unopposed what Grant had also instructed him to do, i.e., "go into the interior of the enemy's country as far as he could, inflicting all the damage he could upon their war resources."[64]

Picture #7
Kurtz painting: "The Four Gun Battery at Resaca"

Harpers Weekly

Picture #8

The campaign in Georgia—Geary's division digging the guns out of a rebel battery before Resaca, on the night of May 15, 1864.

Picture #9

Looking southeast across wagon road to Resaca to battleground of Van der Corput's Confederate four gun battery. The camera position is near the entrenchments occupied by Butterfield's Division of Hooker's XX Army Corps. The village of Resaca is about two miles to the right. It was from this position near these trenches that Butterfield launched his attack on the "Four Gun Battery", May 15, 1864. See the Blakeslee Map sketched May 16, 1864, pages 53 and 54.

Picture #10a
A Lithograph off the Battle of Resaca, GA., May 15, 1864

CHAPTER 7

The Battlefield Abandoned
Sherman Moves South

The following day (May 16) Benjamin Harrison's Indiana regiment remained on the battlefield. It was their duty to aid in burying the dead and collecting the abandoned arms and property of the departed armies.

> The battlefield around Resaca bore evidence of the great struggle that had taken place. Thickets of brush, even great saplings, were literally mown down by the storm of musket balls, shot, shell, grape and canister.[65]

A member of another regiment assigned to the same duty that day noted that

> trees and bushes were barked and slivered in a manner to indicate that the Federal fire had been terrific, especially at the point where the four pieces of artillery had been captured.[66]

Some years after the war, a former officer with the 33rd New Jersey visited the site of his most vivid memory of Resaca:

> ...the little pines were then trees. I found the salient where the battery was, and near it a great long open trench, evidently not a breastwork, for the earth was thrown from it on either side. "What is this?" I asked of the native guide; "This was not here when we fought the battle." "Oh no," said he, "the Yanks buried their dead in that trench. A few years ago they took them up and reburied them in the National Cemetery at Marietta." I have an old canteen with a bullet crease on one side, which I picked up at the open trench that day. Very likely the bullet which creased the canteen killed the man who was carrying it, and the canteen was buried with him in the ditch, and when the bodies were removed, it was left on the ground.[67]

All things considered, the immediate gains achieved by the Union forces at Resaca hardly compensated the common soldier for the effort and suffering he was called upon to make. Many of the best and bravest were casualties. Examined alone, without the benefit of the overall success of the Atlanta Campaign, Resaca should add no luster to Sherman's reputation. In a battle in which casualties exceeded those at First Manassas (Bull Run), in a contest in which a foe, so numerically inferior that it must match divisions against corps, escaped almost certain disaster, Sherman would be acclaimed a tactical genius. It is on this point that the analogy between McClellan at Antietam and Sherman at Resaca breaks down historically: McClellan was discredited; Sherman was congratulated.

The overall success of Sherman's leadership in the final campaigns of the war is the basis for his lofty position as a great military leader. Yet somewhere in the evolving process of enshrining this leader famed for his march through Georgia, we have equated his capture of Atlanta and Savannah with a flare for tactical command that Sherman neither claimed nor his field record warranted. From First Manassas to Bentonville, at Shiloh, Chickasaw Bayou and Missionary Ridge, in tactical situations requiring dash, élan, determination, a certain intuitive sense for timing, place, and moment; a killer instinct—qualities usually associated with great combat leaders—Sherman consistently demonstrated mediocrity. Perhaps Sherman's success in capturing Atlanta has helped us forget that despite a numerical advantage of nearly two-to-one over his opponent, he failed to crush the army he had been sent to destroy. Among the battles he fought and should have won but didn't, yet were credited as victories, is Resaca. Ironically, writers through the years have contributed to the myth by blaming Sherman's subordinates, or the craftiness of his Confederate counterpart for whatever qualifying they must place on his "victory" at Resaca. In a very real sense, the escape of the Confederate army from the trap at Resaca was a major strategic defeat for Sherman. Nevertheless in fairness to Sherman, when reminded once again of his tactical limitations by the Resaca experience, he made major revisions in his plan for the Georgia campaign. He reverted to his proven strength—that of master raider.

Today, despite the encroachments of a modern interstate highway, the scars of battle remain on the hills near Resaca—mute testimony to the contest waged there so long ago. Here, time-worn breastworks, including a chest-deep earthen embrasure where a future American president would lead his Indiana soldiers in a dramatic and successful effort to capture a Confederate artillery battery, a few iron and lead relics from field and woods, and several surviving photographs from the work of Civil War photographer George Barnard who in 1864 captured for eternity the tragedy of the isolated soldier's grave amidst a battle-scared landscape, combine to hallow this ground. Such impressions from a field of battle remind us of the drama of such events, but they can also teach us how the course of history sometimes spins and turns on moments of fleeting opportunities. Here at Resaca, the frustrations and shattered hopes of a military commander for a quick decision rather than the prospect of an uncertain result in a distant future were played out. When Sherman's victorious army marched into Atlanta on September 2, it was largely the result of a long campaign of maneuver attended throughout with great uncertainties. Though, in retrospect, some of his reputation as a great commander seems unwarranted, Sherman deserves credit for his resourcefulness in adjusting his plan of campaign to the nature of the army he commanded and to his own limitations. For Sherman, caught in a fleeting moment of enthusiasm for an uncharacteristic daring plan to destroy his opponent in one bold stroke, Resaca had indeed been a moment of truth.

PART II

Resaca Rediscovered

CHAPTER 8

With the Passing of Time

May 15, 1864

At about 10 P.M. on this day we moved out of our trenches and
began our retreat from the blood-dyed hills of Resaca, and not a
heart but heaved a sigh of regret at abandoning a spot where we had
struggled so hard for thirty-six hours for our common country's
cause—a spot consecrated by the life-blood of so many of the best
and bravest of our comrades in arms; but as we looked for the last
time upon their graves, and knew that the vandal foe would tread
upon them on to-morrow (we felt) that they had not fallen in vain.

R.P. McKelvaine,
Colonel Commanding
24th Mississippi Regiment

In the years following the writing of these heartfelt words by a
Confederate officer in a battle report, the details of the events associated with the struggle between the contending armies at Resaca,
Georgia, were largely forgotten by all but a few. From time to time the
aging veterans of the battle and their families would visit the site, and
on one such occasion a stone marker was erected on the field in honor
of the 103rd Ohio Regiment of Cox's division near the spot of the
failed attack on Confederate entrenchments on May 14, 1864. This
marker is believed to be the only one to have been placed on the field
by battle veterans or by their friends or relatives.

Visiting the Resaca battlefield in the years following the Civil War
was made especially convenient by the continuing operation of the
state-owned railroad connecting Chattanooga and Atlanta—the
wartime Western and Atlantic Railroad. For many years the directing
officials of the railroad promoted passenger travel between Atlanta and

Picture #11
The Norton-Jones House, c. 1860, Resaca, Georgia
This sturdy gothic-style brick house is the only surviving structure from wartime Resaca. It is thought to have been used as a military field hospital after the battle.

Picture #12
Ernest Rutledge, Resaca, Georgia - 1997
Ernest Rutledge at his home overlooking the Resaca battlefield in 1997. The tobacco pipe in his hand led him to the discovery of the battlefield grave on the I-75 construction right of way 37 years ago.

Chattanooga by means of detailed and colorful tourist pamphlets which extolled the opportunities for visiting historical points of interest associated with the 1864 Atlanta Campaign.

Among other activities associated with the immediate post-war history of the Resaca battlefield was the graves recovery effort by the Federal government searching the fields and woods for the scattered burial sites of *Union* soldiers. A corresponding effort was made at this time by local citizens and state officials searching for the remains of Confederate casualties. The Federal government went about this task by letting contracts to private contractors on a "cash bounty per remains" basis with very little field supervision by officials of the work of the individual contractors. As a result, the remains of soldiers were often haphazardly identified as to Federal or Confederate (uniform coat buttons were usually the basis), and sometimes in their hurry to gather the remains and collect the bounty not all the skeletal parts available at the site were included by the contractor in the burial box. The box was then taken to the nearest national cemetery for certification and bounty collection. Thus, because of poor government supervision, and because of real on-site identification difficulties in the field (unless purchased privately or fashioned by the soldier, there were no individual metal "dog tags" in that war), and the occasional practice by individual soldiers in the two armies of wearing uniform components, i.e., military buttons, etc. of standard issue in the opposing army, the intermingling of Union and Confederate dead in national cemetery internment was inevitable.

The cost of collecting Confederate remains at the Resaca battlefield and other battlefields in the South was borne locally with some help from state level funding. Largely though, the effort to recover the Confederate dead was accomplished through the initiative of local citizens, quite often under the leadership of wives, mothers, and sisters of the fallen. As a direct result of these efforts by Southern women the Confederate Cemetery at Resaca was established. Similar cemeteries sprang up throughout the South. Ultimately, these hallowed burial grounds honoring the memory of those who had fallen fighting for the "lost cause" resulted in the official designation in many states of April 26 as Confederate Memorial Day each year in the South.

The deep emotions stirred by such activities may be exemplified best by a notice that appeared in the January, 1898, issue of the *Confederate Veteran Magazine:*

> J. Earl Preston, Esq., of Navasota, Tex.:
>
> At the battle near Resaca, Ga., in the campaign from Dalton to Atlanta, the Forty-Second Alabama, Baker's Brigade (Stewart's Division, Hood's Corps), was engaged. Lieut. Col. [Thomas C.] Lanier, commanding regiment, Capt. McNeil (Company A) acting as major, First Lieut. T.P. Preston, commanding Company A (Hood's Corps) made the celebrated, although unsuccessful, charge on Sherman's breastworks. My brother was mortally wounded near the breastworks. He was taken prisoner, and sent to a Federal field hospital. The surgeon who dressed his wounds, at the request of my brother, wrote to another brother, Hon. S. S. Preston, of Wilson County, Tenn., to send him some money and clothing, which was promptly done, in care of the Federal surgeon, whose name is not remembered.
>
> Nothing more has ever been heard of Lieut. Preston, except he died of his wounds. His widow (now dead) soon after the war went to Resaca and visited the battle-field, to see if she could locate his grave. There were the usual trenches into which the killed were tumbled and covered with Georgia soil, but no mark or name showed who the patriots were. This good wife could never find her husband's grave. If that surgeon is living, we would be gratified to hear from him. He amputated my brother's leg.

In 1960, the remains of a Confederate soldier were unearthed from a trench on Polk's battlefield less than one-half mile east of the Federal hospital behind Bald Hill—an iron tourniquet buckle was in place just above one knee; the leg at the ankle having been amputated. (See battlefield burial site photo next page)

In the more than a century and a quarter since the battle in 1864, remarkably little has changed in the physical appearance of this battle-field. The village of Resaca today remains small, and several families in the community can trace their ancestors to those living in the vicinity in 1864. Small farms and cattle pastures comprise the land use today of much of the battle area—a timber company is in business at the site of Cox and Judah's battles of May 14 near the angle, and modest

Picture #13

Battlefield Burial at Resaca. Remains of a soldier buried in a trench on Polk's Battlefield. This long-forgotten grave was discovered by Ernest Rutledge of Resaca in 1960 directly in the path of construction of Interstate I-75. Rutledge discovered the remains while searching for battlefield artifacts just ahead of the bulldozers. The grave contained a nice brass-lined bowl tobacco pipe, a few bullets near where a pocket had been, and an iron tournequet buckle just above an amputated foot. Could these have been the remains of Confederate Lt. T. P. Preston, whose wounded leg was amputated in a field hospital and his body buried in a nearby trench? (See *Confederate Veteran Magazine,* January, 1898.) Rutledge reburied the remains in the Confederate Cemetary at Resaca.

houses scattered around the area provide homes for many who are employed in nearby Dalton and Calhoun in the carpet industry.

By mid-point in the 20th Century, with the passing of the veterans of the Civil War and their immediate families, public interest in the Civil War was ebbing despite the romantic triumph of the movie *Gone With the Wind* in 1939. Even the scholarly and readable works of popular authors Douglas Southall Freeman and Bell I. Wiley failed to stir the public. The American Civil War Centennial experience (1960-1965) however would change all that.

The Centennial commemoration contributed significantly to the growth of Civil War Round Table organizations throughout the nation, and Civil War reenactor and living history groups were formed and participated in the highly publicized staging of military, social, and political events associated with the War. From these experiences a new generation of Americans discovered the high adventure and tragedy of a nation in the throes of a great struggle for political survival one hundred years earlier. The Civil War centennial commemoration was also the genesis for the birth of the current multi-billion dollar spending spree that has consumed the energies and capital of millions of Americans, and which has promoted the frantic entrepreneurship of thousands of suppliers who strive constantly to satisfy these ever-growing demands for publications, uniforms, battlefield artifacts, and tours. Among these thousands of Civil War enthusiasts are the battlefield "relic hunters"—men and women of all ages who find the "big thrill" of history in the recovery of a lost bullet, buckle, or bayonet from a long forgotten field of battle.

The Resaca battlefield became a favorate hunting ground for such artifacts almost from the beginning. Veterans of the battle returned after the war to revisit the scene of the struggle and often returned from the tour with some item, a cannon ball or canteen (See page 63), as tangible proof of their visit. Local residents tell of picking up quantities of bullets and shell fragments over the years. According to some, bullet holes in earthen trenches could still be seen as late as the 1920's and 1930's and "doodle-bug" exploring of the hole would sometimes uncover a lead bullet "just right for a sinker on your fishing line." Fifty years ago the clearing of a "new ground for crop cultivation" on Polk's battlefield (about where the "Flying J" truck stop is today) furnished young Ernest Rutledge the opportunity to fill his pockets "to the brim" with lead bullets, and shell fragments were everywhere. Years later, employed as an engineer with the Georgia Highway Department, Rutledge would discover a battlefield burial directly in the path of the construction of Interstate 75. (See photo of site, page 75).

It would be the military technology of World War II that would change the "happen chance" discovery of a battlefield artifact to a new hobby of systematic "search and find"—the invention of the land mine detector. By 1946, the military mine detector would be available to the serious battlefield relic hunter, and despite the 30 pound battery pack to power it and the unwieldly wand and cumbersome detecting head, it was a major breakthrough in the successful search for "battlefield iron." Since this detector was so difficult to manage under typical terrain conditions, and since it could not signal non-ferrous metal (lead, etc.) under normal conditions, the demand for something better stimulated the arrival of a new generation of detectors that appeared on the market during the 1950s. These metal detectors weighed less than 10 pounds, were easily repaired, and could detect *all* metals and at greater depths. Battlefield artifact hunting had now arrived in grand style!

The by-products of this new generation of battlefield souvenir hunting were several—some positive and some negative. While most relic hunters obtained permission from the landowner to hunt on private property, some did not and these, sometimes acting carelessly and irresponsibly, did damage to fields and woods by failing to refill their "dig holes" or by leaving behind food wrapper and container litter. Though most relic hunters were responsible and most restricted their hunting to private property (and 80% of the 10,000 Civil War battlefields are such), some trespassing and poaching on national and state historic sites did take place. Penalties for such activities have increased in severity over the years so that today these violations are negligible. The most positive and significant by-product from this interest in battlefield artifacts is the emergence of a group of technical historians often very good at their work, and becoming increasingly better in terms of accurate and rather sophisticated information regarding military equipment and its use. Often fired by a money-driven practical interest in a *successful* search for war artifacts in the field, they have become experts regarding weapons, battle terrain, ammunition, military accoutrements, tactical movements, and the verification of troop positions in the field. These people have scoured private collections, archives, estate sales, and flea markets and have accumulated an impressive quantity of reliable information, often cross- referenced, and frequently site-verified to a particular battlefield. The alert academician will take note of this accumulating body of information and make use of it. In the following pages several of these "non traditional" historians will share some experiences and observations resulting from years of field study at Resaca and other sites of battle in the Civil War.

CHAPTER 9

A Century Later—New Interest

LARRY THORNTON lives in Dalton, Georgia, where he is engaged in the insurance business. Thornton is a decorated Vietnam veteran having earned the Silver Star while serving two tours of duty with the Army Special Forces. He is college educated and has studied law. His interest in the Resaca area began more than twenty years ago. Since then he has continued to expand his study always focusing on battle and camp at this and other fields of combat in the Civil War. Specializing in searching primary source materials followed by extensive battlefield visits, Thornton has accumulated much information, and currently is engaged in transferring this data to computer file. He is well known for his interest in the Atlanta Campaign, becoming something of a switchboard for the exchange of battlefield information in north Georgia. In the past twenty years he has spent hundreds of hours on the Resaca battlefield verifying documentary information. His tools in the field include good maps, a shovel, a metal detector, and a notebook.

Polk's Battlefield At Resaca
Action Near Bald Hill

THORNTON'S STATEMENT: "Having done some insurance work for Weems Brown (property owner of a substantial portion of the south end of the battlefield near the Confederate position commanded by General Leonidas Polk), Mr. Brown allowed me to hunt in his pasture near the creek (Camp Creek) and the hills nearby. This was in the early 1970s and at that time I had only limited research sources of information about the action here and so it was confusing to see an array of picket holes and infantry trenches on both sides of the hill. There was even a battery position (artillery) on this hill near Mr.

Picture #14
Larry Thornton

Jack Melton

Ernest Rutledge

Resaca Battlefield Historians

Brown's house. There were quantities of Confederate Enfield bullets of English manufacture imbedded in the east face of this hill and quantities of "three-ringers" (Federal fired and unfired ammunition) on the top and west side of the hill."

SUMMARY NOTE

Thornton gradually sorted through the information he had accumulated on the site (his document research, maps, the recovered artifacts and their locations, etc.) and concluded that the combined evidence suggested this hill near Weems Brown's house had been occupied first by Confederates, and that certain existing trenches facing west had been "turned" (that is, reconstructed in reverse) by the Federals so that they faced the main Confederate positions on the hills east of the creek). He concluded that Confederate sharpshooters had been targeting this hill because Whitworth rifle bullets (special sharpshooter bullets used only by the Confederates) were found nearby. Behind this hill there was a hollow where quantities of dropped Federal rifle bullets were found, suggesting an ammunition replenishment area, and nearby he found evidence that a house had once been located on that particular site. Because of so much battlefield action nearby, Thornton called this place "Haunted Hollow."

Polk's Battlefield Hills On East Bank of Camp Creek:

THORNTON: "On the east side of the old creek bed (where the creek has been rerouted somewhat by locals in recent years) several small hills rise sharply. These hills contain picket holes and shallow trenches on both east and west sides. Deep infantry trenches and several cannon emplacements are also found here with some evidence that several of these trenches had been reversed (see note above) to face the main Confederate defenses nearer town (Resaca). (See position Map #2 from *The Official Military Atlas of the Civil War*). My research indicated that the Marion Artillery (Florida) was originally in action on these hills (A.J. Neal's Diary and Thornton's field study), but that it had been repositioned nearer town prior to the Federal attack on these hills on the east bank of the creek. The attack received flank fire from Hardee's and Polk's lines northeast of the path of the movement. The recovery of numerous Colt pistol bullets near this junction of Hardee's and Polk's lines indicate a serious effort had been made to carry the position or at least to silence this threat to the Union flank. What ultimately became the main battleground in Polk's front after the capture of the hills at the creek was the quarter-mile of ground directly eastward from these hills toward the main Confederate defensive line near town. Attack and counterattack took place over those hills and fields (now occupied by the SR 136 overpass at I-75 and the Flying "J" truckstop) until nearly 10 P.M., often at very close range. According to Neal's Diary, a barn was set afire which helped illuminate the battlefield after dark."

SUMMARY NOTE:

Thornton, using the *Official Records* and *The Official Military Atlas of the Civil War,* Neal's Diary, Nisbet's *4 Years on the Firing Line* and other sources, took advantage of a unique opportunity a few years ago to search the fields of Polk's battle after deep grading had taken place (two to three foot depths) in preparation for the construction of the truck stop ("Flying J") near I-75. He came to the conclusion that some heavy fighting at close quarters had indeed taken place there. Because of continued farming and frequent river flooding, this relatively flat "bottom land" between the hills and town had received more than a foot of new soil in the years since the battle. It is Thornton's theory that the unusual depth of many of the bullets he recovered here can be accounted for partially by the angle of fire from the hills and the close proximity of the combatants. He offers as evidence several lead rifle bullets and canister shot recovered from this area which were flattened by the force of impact—the result of close range and high angle conditions.

The Battle Action At the Resaca Angle: Cox & Judah's Assault

THORNTON: "The portion of the Confederate line at Resaca occupied by Hardee's Corps was a well-constructed defense system in depth (several parallel lines of earthworks), probably constructed several days prior to the battle by a group of 4000 Confederate soldiers already at Resaca. The ground is slatey and at that particular season was very hard requiring some of the digging to be done with axes—I found several ax heads here. Many of these lines of earthworks were of unusual construction angling at 30 degrees toward the crest of the individual hill so as to give protection from enfilading artillery and rifle fire from the corresponding hills west of Camp Creek. The divisions of Cox and Judah preparing for the assault on Hardee's north/south line where the line joined Hoods Corps' east/west line (creating an angle in the Confederate defenses), assembled near the present day location of Zack Airport. From here they marched to the attack by way of a gully (hollow) protected by low hills. When they broke out at the point of the ridge in the valley where the two branches of Camp Creek join they were checked by an advance line of Confederate infantry dug in on this ridge point. Being exposed simultaneously to a terrific artillery fire from Hotchkiss' battalion of artillery which decimated their ranks, the Federal soldiers took shelter behind the banks of the nearby creek."

SUMMARY NOTE

Thornton's field studies enabled him to track the movements of Federal units involved in this unsuccessful attack at the Angle to an ammunition replenishment point some half mile west of the battle front. Here, Thornton recovered large quantities of unused rifle ammunition. This discovery identifies the destination of Cox's Division when it was relieved to replenish supplies after their fight at the Angle on May 14. Thornton also found data in several wartime or early post-war documents regarding "two or three" iron cannon and four dismounted caissons left in Hardee's line of defense when the Confederate army retired from the field the night of May 15. Thornton speculates that if indeed these cannon were abandoned at Resaca it was because they were old outdated 6-pdr. iron smoothbore guns not worth the effort to carry them further in the retreat southward. This preliminary documentation of the "abandoned cannon at Resaca" though inconclusive, would seem to give some credence to a local tale repeated over the years that "two or three cannon" have been sighted in the river when the water in is low during occasional dry seasons. To date, all efforts to locate these guns have been unsuccessful.

In concluding this July 1996 interview, Thornton was asked to comment on the significance of preserving the Resaca battlefield as a national historical site:

THORNTON: "Resaca was the first major battle of the Atlanta Campaign. Today this battlefield is in pristine condition. Only a few families have owned this land down through the years. Except for the interstate highway (I-75), this land is like the soldiers left it in 1864. The old Lee farm (now the 1200 acre Weaver property the state hopes to purchase) is the prime historic property—it is the neatest piece of land on the battlefield. If we lose this battlefield where so little has changed through the years, we have lost a great piece of history."

ERNEST RUTLEDGE is a life long resident of the Resaca community. He traces his Resaca ancestors back several generations. Rutledge is a retired Georgia Department of Transportation employee who has maintained his roots to this community and its history through the years. He remembers a boyhood growing up in the Resaca area in the 1930s and 1940s, about the abundance of battlefield relics after every "plowing or rain," and how useful such easily available "minie balls" were for lead weights on a fishing line. Rutledge, however, had a unique and enduring sense of history about the Resaca battlefield which carried him beyond boyhood years through life to the present.

Not satisfied with the occasional visual discovery of a battlefield relic, and after a chance meeting on the Resaca battlefield with pioneer relic hunter Ralph Righton who was having a "good day" using the latest in detecting equipment, Rutledge decided to "give up rabbit traps and squirrel hunting" and devote his spare time to "serious" searching for battlefield relics. In the late 1950s, Rutledge was among the first in Georgia to use the new light-weight T-10 metal detector manufactured by the Fischer Company of California. Relying little on "book" research, he chose instead to take advantage of his lifelong familiarity with the locations of forts and trenches on the hills and ridges surrounding his home community and simply begin digging. As detecting equipment technology improved with the passing years, Rutledge's battlefield collection grew rapidly. Perhaps the most unusual experience was the discovery of a trench burial on the Resaca battlefield. (See Picture 13, page 75).

RUTLEDGE: "As an employee with the Georgia Department of Transportation, I became involved with the construction of Interstate 75 in 1960. Several hills and ridges near the Oostanaula River just west of town (Resaca) were being removed in the grading work required to construct the highway. Several of these hills served as barrow pits furnishing the supply of dirt needed to build the ramps required by the intersection of State Highway 136 and I-75. Most of these hills contained well preserved trenchworks. I discovered one of these hills contained a military burial site.

The burial site was in a trench on one of the hills scheduled to be removed in a day or two for construction purposes. Aware of this, I began a careful metal detecting on this hill after finishing my work for the highway department one day and found a clay tobacco pipe with a quarter inch brass band near the top of the pipe bowl; nearby at about an eight inch depth lay a large bone. A state archaeologist (Dan Morse) working at an Indian mound near the river (Oostanaula) a half mile south examined the bone and thought it to be human. I told him (Morse) that I wanted to finish the excavation of this burial site myself and he quickly taught me the basic procedures of brush and sifting screen. Late the next day I began the work. I had brought my Shepherd dog along and as I started to continue this dig, with daylight fading, I was startled to see the dog immediately take a stance a few feet from where I had found the bone and, pointing his nose to the sky, began howling—something he had never done before. Several days were required to uncover the burial. Aside from some unfired minie balls and a rifle tampion (a device used to plug the muzzle of a musket to keep moisture out of the barrel), there were only a few buttons of bone or rubber (underwear buttons?) found. And there was one other thing, *a small iron tourniquet buckle just above the right knee, and the unmistakable marks left by a saw on the bone just above the ankle—the right foot was missing!*"

SUMMARY NOTE

Rutledge's experiences relating to the discovery of the battlefield burial continued for several years. Authentication of the remains by archaeologists, a coroner's inquest, a futile search for authority to bury the remains in the Resaca Confederate Cemetery, a "near burial" in the wrong cemetery in another city, several years of "lost and found" storage of the remains at a local mortuary, and the storage of these same remains at his personal home, left Rutledge understandably somewhat frustrated. Finally, through persistence, after encountering years of bureaucratic indecision and indifference by private and public authorities, he buried the remains of this soldier in the Confederate Cemetery at Resaca.

JACK MELTON lives in Marietta, Georgia in 1997. He is an author and technical specialist in field artillery projectiles of the Civil War. As a child he became interested in military relics when he found his first cannonball near his home in the 1970s. His early interest in artillery projectile technology led him to become acquainted with noted collector Thomas Dickey (deceased 1987) of Atlanta and this association resulted in Melton's scholarly pursuit for accurate information. Through patent research at the National Archives, and through measuring and photographing projectile specimens recovered from Civil War battlefields, Melton has contributed much to our technical knowledge concerning artillery ammunition. He is the author of several publications on the subject. His work has done much to correct errors in earlier publications having to do with performance, field use, and the manufacturing of specific types of field artillery ammunition.

JACK MELTON: "The most frustrating task I face in writing my books has been sorting through existing publications (primary and secondary materials) which are often filled with inaccuracies and conflicting information. Locating patent information at the National Archives was a great step forward toward correcting much misinformation, and having the opportunity to share research data gathered by others whose battlefield artifact recoveries and trading interests have led them to search out the factory records of ammunition-producing arsenals and proving grounds, has been invaluable.

"In addition to practicing research skills 'learned on the job,' I have also learned camera skills. My first book, *Introduction to Field Artillery Ordnance, 1861-1865* is subtitled *A Pictorial Study of Civil War Artillery Projectiles* which suggests the need for high quality photographs—a professional skill I had to learn to make publication financially possible. A good camera, professional tips, and a lot of practice and patience eventually brought results. Today I may have the largest and best indexed collection of photographs on the subject of field artillery ammunition in the country. I hope so, because with this photographic collection and with my published work, I would like to think that I have carried on this study in a manner my friend and mentor Tom Dickey would have approved."

CHAPTER 10

Construction of Interstate–75

In August 1959, Dan F. Morse, an archaeologist with the Georgia Highway Department, became aware that portions of the Resaca Civil War entrenchments were to be destroyed by the construction of Interstate-75. A contract was made between the Federal Highway Archaeology Salvage Program and the State Highway Department to allow eleven weeks of excavation. The work was done in the summer of 1960 and a written report was made by Cecil B. Cook, Jr., Highway Salvage Archaeologist, to the Georgia Historical Commission regarding the results of this field study. Beverly Dubose, representing the Georgia Historical Commission is cited in the report and thanked by the archaeologist for "his advice and encouragement, (and for) his on-the-spot explanations of the engagements fought at Resaca and use of his extensive library on the Civil War."

Perhaps the most disappointing aspect of the Morse/Cook study was that the entire field excavation focused primarily on the Confederate trenches at the point of the intersection of Hood's and Hardee's lines. The greatest damage to the battlefield by the highway construction was not at that point but instead on Polk's front at the south end of the field where a half-mile swathe of small battle ridges and hills were removed in the process of constructing the interstate ramps necessary to access State Route 136. In Cook's report, he explains this omission by stating: "Unfortunately, the southernmost Federal trench resting on the Oostanaula River (Polk's battlefield) was literally torn to pieces by avid collectors before excavations commenced at Resaca in May, 1960." A surprising statement since today, thirty-seven years later, on the remaining hills not destroyed by the highway construction, one can see well preserved earthworks in abundance. In 1960, long before the advent of today's crowds of avid collectors, Polk's battlefield was largely intact. Some usual "wear and tear" caused by a century of normal agricultural activities was of course to be expected. Whatever the reason for neglecting this portion of the field, we know that an opportunity to learn more about this now vanished battle site of May 14, 1864, on Polk's front, through careful field study and mapping, has been irretrievably lost.

Cook continued his report by describing the location and relationship of Federal and Confederate earthworks on the Resaca field:

> The right-of-way of Interstate Route 75 interrupts Federal and Confederate trenches in four places; moving from the Oostanaula River north, (1) a Federal trench running perpendicular to the River one half a mile due west of Resaca, (2) the Confederate line an equal distance northwest of Resaca where it turns eastward coming down off the hills bordering the east of Camp Creek, (3) the Confederate trenches at the northern angle where the line bends back northeast and (4) a Federal trench across one of the small tributaries making up Camp Creek.... The second line of trenches making up the Confederate line as it turns away from Camp Creek toward Resaca were almost obliterated by plowing, so that Mr. Morse did not detect them when surveying the battlefield. Authorization to spend Federal funds on this portion of the right-of-way to salvage these trenches was therefore not included in the contract with the State Highway Department.

Cook then goes on to describe the work of the archaeological excavation conducted by Morse and himself at the angle of the Confederate breastworks, as well as their work in excavating an opposing line of Federal breastworks across Camp Creek some 2000 yards farther to the northwest. In the vicinity of the Confederate angle they:

> dug the remains of a cannon emplacement overlooking Camp Creek valley, an associated line of trenches, two empty Federal (?) graves in front of the main lines and a Union "fox hole" (rifle pit) across the creek in the rear of the Federal trench. The second series of excavations explored two trenches diverging to the south away from the cannon emplacements at the angle and a possible second series of cannon emplacements thirty yards to the southwest in a small partially protected hollow. Four possible picket posts were excavated in advance of the main lines at the angle, being concentrated about 300 feet to the northeast on the downward

slope of the hill facing out over Camp Creek valley. One disinterred grave, identified as such by two eagle buttons found in the fill, was also excavated 100 feet to the west of the picket posts mentioned. One hundred and fifty feet of the Federal trench on the opposing ridge was excavated and the remaining 150 feet falling within the right-of-way tested by 10 foot wide trenches at 25 foot intervals. Two Federal fox holes a few feet in advance of the main line and one in the rear were also dug. A dugout or "hidy hole" in the rear of the Confederate main line was dug to the south of the angle on the back side of a hill fronting on Camp Creek, and four rifle pits further to the south and behind the lines were dug.

Typical of a traditional archaeological study such as this, the yield in battlefield artifacts was not great:

> 1 bayonet from embankment of western most trench diverging from the cannon emplacements at the angle; 1 live 3" Hotchkiss shell in the embankment of the supposed second cannon emplacement at the angle (seems to have been fired from the north over the high point of the angle); almost the complete metal hardware of a knapsack, its contents, and the metal eyes from a pair of boots beside the two graves dug earlier by Morse; several badly mutilated cartridge boxes, bayonet scabbard tip from the Federal trench; 2 eagle buttons from a Federal (?) grave in front of the Confederate angle; and quantities of shell fragments and minie balls.

Cook's conclusions about which Confederate units were at the focal points of Judah's and Cox's attacks on the 14th, and what the exact positions of Hotchkiss' and Martin's Confederate batteries were at the point of the angle, are in general agreement with standard studies of this battle action. Nothing of great significance was added to our knowledge of the battle of Resaca with this archaeological study by the State Highway Department in 1960. The solid field work of the earlier research at Resaca done by historians Beverly Dubose, Ralph Righton, and Wilbur Kurtz in the 1950s was neither substantially augmented nor diminished by the 1960 field study—little new information was added to our knowledge of the battlefield, and the portion of the field (Polk's battle front) most stressed by the construction of the highway was not included in the study.

Traditional archaeological projects such as the Resaca study are labor intensive and time consuming, and thus very expensive. What we are learning is that there is practical value in a professionally controlled and supervised field study combining archaeologists trained in military history with volunteer assistants equipped with modern metal detecting devices. Such a team can cover a much wider area in a shorter time, and by accumulating a greater variety of artifacts and associated information, result in a more representative picture of the battle action on the field and of the soldiers involved in the event.

The impact of I-75 on the Resaca battlefield has had some negative effects. While the presence of the highway gives easy access to the historic ground and thus encourages tourism and educational use, with the erasing by highway construction of the substantial entrenchments at the interchange of SR136 and I-75 nearly a half mile of unrecorded field works were lost. The absence here on Polk's battlefield of a satisfactory study before highway construction, has subsequently led to factual mistakes and mapping errors in published works regarding troop positions and battle action at Resaca. Several such mistakes have today gained common acceptance among some historians and with much of the public.

Since there is no highway interchange at the Hood/Hardee angle, the destruction of entrenchments here by road construction is a less serious matter than at Polk's portion of the battlefield. The width of the damage here is limited to the footprint of the highway and the associated slopes. And since a report of the 1960 archaeological study of this part of the field has survived the years, it would seem we have cause to be grateful—and so we are. But how nice it would have been if highway design engineers and Civil War historians had become acquainted sooner!

An Epilogue

In the summer of 1997 purchase of the 1200 acres of battlefield at Resaca seems imminent. This acreage (almost half the size of Kennesaw Mountain National Battlefield Park) includes the majority of the battle site at the Angle (see map overlay), and a portion of the field of action at Polk's battle location. These acres constitute roughly 60% of the total field of battle at Resaca and encompass the location of some of the heaviest fighting on May 14-15, 1864. Considered the dramatic core area of the battlefield, these acres contain quantities of military entrenchments. Many of these fortifications have unusual construction alignments relative to terrain (i.e., Hardee's Confederate defenses). These unique defenses achieve a greater military strength by being constructed at right angles to the Federal entrenchments when the natural shoulders and contours of ridges so dictate.

Enhancing the value of this historic property is the existence of 1864 photographic documentation concentrating on the line of terrain and fortifications along the Camp Creek portion of the battlefield. This is the work of photographer George Barnard who accompanied Sherman during the latter part of the Atlanta Campaign. A comparison of Barnard's wartime photographs with comparable camera angles today indicates that little has changed over the years at Resaca with regard to relative location of fields, timbered ridges, and streams. By comparing these 1864 photographs with views today we are given an opportunity here at Resaca to create in a sense a time-bridge—to visually transport the visitor through a unique and dramatic experience—to figuratively experience a walk with Colonel McKelvaine of the 24th Mississippi Regiment through his "BLOOD-DYED HILLS OF RESACA; A SPOT CONSECRATED BY THE LIFE-BLOOD OF SO MANY OF THE BEST AND BRAVEST"— an opportunity to reflect on the higher lessons learned and the values gained from such tragic episodes in human history.

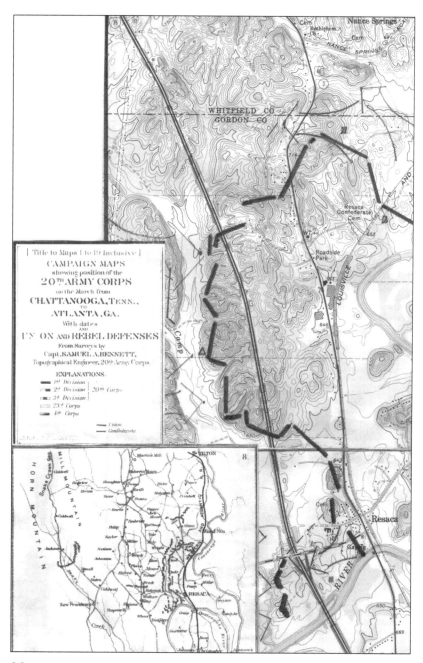

Map #12a
Resaca Field of Battle

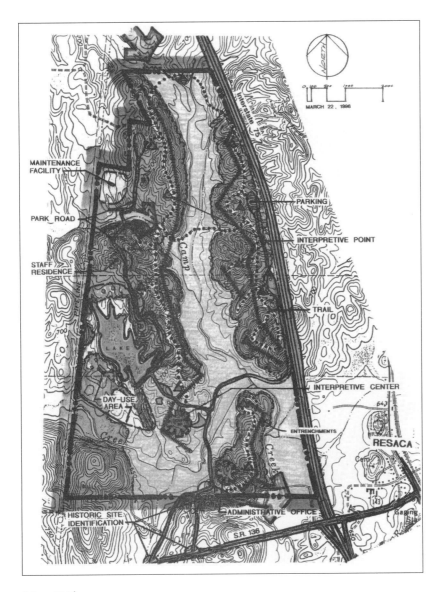

Map #12b
Conceptual Development Plan for the Resaca Historic Civil War battlefield site.
Gordon County, Georgia *(The Georgia Civil War Commission)* Map overlay

1 *War of the Rebellion: A Compilation of the Official Records of the Union and Confederate Armies* (Washington, D.C., 1880-1901), Series I, Vol. 38, pt.1, p.115; pt.3, p.676. (Hereafter cited as *Official Records.*)

2. William T. Sherman, (quoted), Joseph M. Brown, *Western & Atlantic Railroad* (Atlanta: Western & Atlantic Railroad, 1887) 40.

3. Jacob Dolson Cox, *Atlanta* (New York: Charles Scribner's Sons, 1882) 31.

4. *Official Records,* Series I, Vol. 38, pt. 4, p. 39-40.

5. Ibid., pt. 4, p. 25.

6. Ibid., p. 40.

7. Ibid., pt. 1, p. 257.

8. Ibid., pt. 4, p. 663.

9. Ibid., pt.3, pp.721, 874, 398, 614; James Cooper Nisbet, *4 Years on the Firing Line* (Jackson, Tennessee: McCowart-Mercer, 1963; originally published 1914) 179.

10. *Official Records,* Series I, Vol. 38, pt. 3, p. 375.

11. Ibid., 90.

12. Ibid., 16; pt. 4, p. 40; William T. Sherman, *Memoirs of General William T. Sherman* (New York: Charles L. Webster & Co., 1875) 33-34.

13. Nisbet, *4 Years,* p. 179; *Official Records,* Series I, vol. 38, pt. 3, p. 398.

14. *Official Records,* Series I, vol. 38, pt. 3, p. 376.

15. *Ibid.*

16. Ibid.; Nisbet, *4 Years,* 179.

17. *Official Records,* Series I, vol. 38, pt. 3, p. 376.

18. Jacob D. Cox Diary, 13 May 1864 (typed manuscript, Kennesaw Mountain National Battlefield Park, Kennesaw, Georgia. (Hereinafter cited as Cox's Diary).

19. Stephen Pierson, "From Chattanooga to Atlanta in 1864—A Personal Reminiscence," *Proceedings of the New Jersey Historical Society, A Quarterly Magazine* (July, 1931), 7-8.

20. Jacob D. Cox, *Military Reminiscences of the Civil War* (New York: C. Scribner's Sons, 1900), 2:216; Cox's Diary, 13 May 1864.

21. Cox, *Reminiscences,* 2:216.

22. *Official Records,* Series I, vol. 38, pt. 1, p. 521.

23. Ibid., p.220.

24. Oliver O. Howard, *Autobiography of Oliver Otis Howard* (New York: Baker & Taylor Co., 1907), 1:511.

25. Cox, *Reminiscences,* 2:221.

26. *Official Records,* Series I, vol. 38, pt. 3, p. 811; Wilbur G. Kurtz, Resaca Field Map #1 (author's possession).

27. William J. McMurray, *History of the Twentieth Tennessee Regiment Volunteer Infantry, C.S.A.* (Nashville: W.J. McMurray, 1904) 309-310.

28. *Official Records,* Series I, vol.38, pt. 3, p. 722.

29. McMurray, Twentieth Tennessee, 310; *Official Records,* Series I, vol. 38, pt. 3, p. 796. See also Craig Symonds, *Stonewall of the West: Patrick Cleburne and the Civil War* (Lawrence: University Press of Kansas, 1987) 206-207.

30. Edwin H. Reynolds, *A History of the Henry County Commands Which Served in the Confederate States Army* (Kennesaw, Georgia: Continental Book Co., 1961; originally published 1904) 76.

31. *Official Records,* Series I, vol. 38, pt. 3, pp. 801-2.

32. Charles A. Partridge, ed., *History of the 96th Regiment Illinois Volunteer Infantry* (Chicago: Brown-Pettibone & Co., 1887) 321-2.

33. Ibid.

34. Ibid.

35. Ibid.; *Official Records,* Series I, vol. 38, pt. 1, pp. 488-9

36. *Official Records,* Series I, vol. 38, pt. 3, pp. 91, 142, 190, 377.

37. Ibid., 126.

38. Ibid., 126-7, 142.

39. Nisbet, *4 Years,* 179-180.

40. *Official Records*, Series I, vol. 38, pt. 3, p. 93.

41. Ibid., 191.

42. Nisbet, *4 Years,* 181.

43. *Official Records*, Series I, vol. 38, pt. 3, p. 143.

44. Ibid., pt. 4, pp.189, 190, 198, 200.

45. Ibid., 165.

46. Ibid., pt. 3, pp. 377, 420-1, 615, 817.

47. Ibid., 615; pt. 4, p. 716.

48. Ibid., pt. 4, p. 716.

49. Ibid., pt. 3, p. 813.

50. Ibid.

51. *Confederate Veteran Magazine* (January, 1898) 15.

52. *Official Records*, Series I, vol. 38, pt. 3, pp. 839-40.

53. Ibid.

54. Howard, *Autobiography,* 1:516.

55. *Official Records*, Series I, vol. 38, pt. 1, pp. 190-1; Cox's Diary, 15 May 1864.

56. *Official Records*, Series I, vol. 38, pt. 2, p. 366; pt. 3, pp. 812-813.

57. Ibid.

58. Howard, *Autobiography,* 1:517.

59. *Official Records*, Series I, vol. 38, pt. 2, p. 371.

60. Howard, *Autobiography,* 1:517; *Official Records*, Series I, vol. 38, pt. 2, p. 366

61. Pierson, "From Chattanooga to Atlanta," 12-13.

62. Partridge, ed., *96th Regiment,* 328.

63. John R. Boyle, *Soldiers True* (New York: Eaton & Mains, 1903) 207.

64. *Official Records*, Series I, vol. 38, pt. 4, p. 40.

65. James Barnes, et.al., *The 86th Regiment Indiana Volunteer Infantry* (Crawfordville, Indiana: Journal Company Printers, 1895) 347.

66. Partridge, ed., *96th Regiment,* 333.

67. Pierson, "From Chattanooga to Atlanta," 13.

Barnes, James, et.al. *The 86th Regiment Indiana Volunteer Infantry.* Crawfordville, Indiana, 1895.

Boyle, John R. *Soldiers True.* New York, 1903.

Brown, Joseph M. *Western & Atlantic Railroad.* Atlanta, 1887.

Casteel, Albert. *Decision in the West: The Atlanta Campaign of 1864.* Lawrence: The University Press of Kansas, 1992.

Cox, Jacob Dolson. *Atlanta.* New York, 1882.

_____. *Cox Diary.* Typed manuscript, Kennesaw Mountain National Battlefield Park, Kennesaw, Georgia.

_____. *Military Reminiscences of the Civil War.* New York, 1900.

Confederate Veteran Magazine (January, 1898).

Howard, Oliver Otis. *Autobiography of Oliver Otis Howard.* New York, 1907.

McMurray, William J. *History of the Twentieth Tennessee Volunteer Infantry.* Nashville, 1904.

Nisbet, James Cooper. *4 Years on the Firing Line.* Jackson, Tennessee, 1963 [org. 1914].

Partridge, Charles A., ed. *History of the 96th Regiment Illinois Volunteer Infantry.* Chicago, 1887.

Pierson, Stephen. "From Chattanooga to Atlanta in 1864—A Personal Reminiscence," *Proceedings of the New Jersey Historical Society, A Quarterly Magazine* (July, 1931).

Reynolds, Edwin H. *A History of the Henry County Commands Which Served in the Confederate States Army.* Kennesaw, Georgia, 1961 [orig. 1904].

Sherman, William T. *Memoirs of General William T. Sherman.* New York, 1875.

Symonds, Craig. *Stonewall of the West: Patrick Cleburne and the Civil War.* Lawrence, Kansas, 1997.

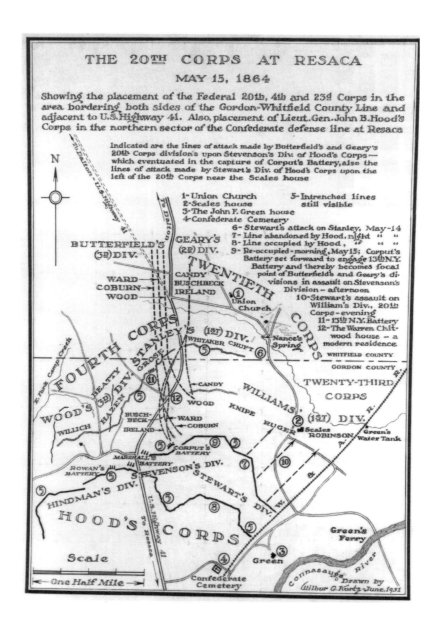

Picture #15
The 20th Corps at Resaca
May 15, 1864

Index

The Battle of Resaca: Atlanta Campaign 1864
Philip L. Secrist

Mercer University Press, Spring 1998
Editor: Marc A. Jolley
Book Design: Jay Polk
Jacket Design: Jim Burt
Text Font: Adobe Garamond
Printed by McNaughton & Gunn, Inc.